The Treasury of Favorite Love Poems

The
Treasury of
Favorite
Love Poems

Permission Acknowledgments

Grateful acknowledgement is made to the following for permission to reprint previously published material; where indicated, such permission is still pending:

For "Carry Her Over the Water", "Leap Before You Look", "Lullaby" and "O Tell Me The Truth About Love" by W.H. Auden, from *W.H. Auden: Collected Poems* by W.H. Auden, edited by Edward Mendelson, copyright © 1940 and renewed 1968 by W.H. Auden: Random House, Inc.

For "She Who Is Always In My Thoughts" by Bhartrhari, translated from the Sanskrit by John Brough, from *Poems from the Sanskrit Translated by John Brough*, copyright © 1968: Penguin Books, Ltd. (pending).

For "A Black Wedding Song" by Gwendolyn Brooks, from *Beckonings* by Gwendolyn Brooks, copyright © 1975: Gwendolyn Brooks (pending).

For "As Sweet" and "Loss" by Wendy Cope, from *Serious Concerns* by Wendy Cope, copyright ©1992: Faber & Faber (pending).

For "i like my body when it is with your", copyright 1923, 1925, 1951, 1953, ©1991 by the Trustees for the E. E. Cummings Trust, copyright ©1976 by George James Firmage, "being to timelessness as it's to time,", copyright 1950, © 1978, 1991 by the Trustees for the E. E. Cummings Trust, "if everything happens that can't be done", copyright 1944, © 1972, 1991 by the Trustees for the E. E. Cummings Trust, by e. e. cummings, from *Selected Poems* by e.e. cummings, Introduction & Commentary Richard S. Kennedy: Liveright Publishing Corporation.

For "Marriage Counsel" by Ruby Dee, from *My One Good Nerve*, edited by Ruby Dee, copyright © 1998: Third World Press (pending).

For "On Marriage" by Kahlil Gibran, from *The Prophet* by Kahlil Gibran, copyright © 1923: Alfred A. Knopf, a division of Random House, Inc.; Gibran National Committee, U.K. and Canada.

For "A Poem of Friendship" by Nikki Giovanni, from *Nikki Giovanni – Love Poems*, copyright © 1997: William Morrow and Co., Inc. (pending).

For "Friday Night" by Robert Graves from *Complete Poems*: Carcanet Press Ltd.

Contents

*New
Love*

New Face

I have learned not to worry about love;
but to honor its coming
with all my heart.
To examine the dark mysteries
of the blood
with headless heed and
swirl,
to know the rush of feelings
swift and flowing
as water.
The source appears to be
some inexhaustible
spring
within our twin and triple
selves;
the new face I turn up
to you
no one else on earth
has ever
seen.

— ALICE WALKER

First Love

I ne'er was struck before that hour
    With love so sudden and so sweet,
Her face it bloomed like a sweet flower
    And stole my heart away complete.
My face turned pale as deadly pale.
    My legs refused to walk away,
And when she looked, what could I ail?
    My life and all seemed turned to clay.

And then my blood rushed to my face
    And took my eyesight quite away,
The trees and bushes round the place
    Seemed midnight at noonday.
I could not see a single thing,
    Words from my eyes did start—
They spoke as chords do from the string,
    And blood burnt round my heart.

Are flowers the winter's choice?
    Is love's bed always snow?
She seemed to hear my silent voice,
    Not love's appeals to know.
I never saw so sweet a face
    As that I stood before.
My heart has left its dwelling-place
    And can return no more.

— JOHN CLARE

Love

Love bade me welcome; yet my soul drew back,
   Guilty of dust and sin.
But quick-eyed Love, observing me grow slack
   From my first entrance in,
Drew nearer to me, sweetly questioning
   If I lacked anything.

"A guest," I answered, "worthy to be here";
   Love said, "You shall be he."
"I, the unkind, ungrateful? Ah, my dear,
   I cannot look on Thee."
Love took my hand, and smiling did reply,
   "Who made the eyes but I?"

"Truth, Lord, but I have marred them; let my
   shame
   Go where it doth deserve."
"And know you not," says Love, "who bore the
   blame?"
   "My dear, then I will serve."
"You must sit down," says Love, "and taste My
   meat."
   So I did sit and eat.

— GEORGE HERBERT

6

Life and Love

Fast this Life of mine was dying,
　　Blind already and calm as death,
Snowflakes on her bosom lying
　　Scarcely heaving with her breath.

Love came by, and having known her
　　In a dream of fabled lands,
Gently stooped, and laid upon her
　　Mystic chrism of holy hands;

Drew his smile across her folded
　　Eyelids, as the swallow dips;
Breathed as finely as the cold did
　　Through the locking of her lips.

So, when Life looked upward, being
　　Warmed and breathed on from above
What sight could she have for seeing,
　　Evermore . . . but only LOVE?

— ELIZABETH BARRETT BROWNING

"It lies not in our power
to love or hate"

It lies not in our power to love or hate,
For will in us is overruled by fate.
When two are stripped, long ere the course begin,
We wish that one should love, the other win;
And one especially do we affect
Of two gold ingots, like in each respect:
The reason no man knows; let it suffice
What we behold is censured by our eyes.
Where both deliberate, the love is slight:
Who ever loved, that loved not at first sight?

— CHRISTOPHER MARLOWE

To—

—She was a lovely one—her shape was light
And delicately flexible; her eye
Might have been black, or blue,—
  but it was bright,
Though beaming not on every passer-by;
'Twas very modest, and a little shy.
The eyelash seemed to shade the very cheek;
That had the color of a sunset sky,
Not rosy—but a soft and heavenly streak
For which the arm might strike—the heart might
  break—
And a soft gentle voice, that kindly sweet
Accosted one she chanced to overtake,
While walking slowly on iambic feet,
In tones that fell as soft as heavens own dew—
Who was it! dear young Lady, was it you?

— JOHN BRAINARD

Somewhere

Somewhere there waiteth in this world of ours
for one lone soul, another lonely soul—
Each chasing each through all the weary hours,
And meeting strangely at one sudden goal;
Then blend they—like green leaves with golden
  flowers,
Into one beautiful and perfect whole—
And life's long night is ended, and the way
Lies open onward to eternal day.

— SIR EDWIN ARNOLD

Medicine Song
of an Indian Lover

I.

Who, maiden, makes this river flow?
The Spirit—he makes its ripples glow—
But I have a charm that can make thee, dear,
Steal o'er the wave to thy lover here.

II.

Who, maiden, makes this river flow?
The Spirit—he makes its ripples glow—
Yet every blush that my love would hide,
Is mirror'd for me in the tell-tale tide.

III.

And though thou shouldst sleep on the
    farthest isle,
Round which these dimpling waters smile—
Yet I have a charm that can make thee, dear,
Steal over the wave to thy lover here.

— OJIBWA

A Birthday

My heart is like a singing bird
   Whose nest is in a water'd shoot;
My heart is like an apple-tree
   Whose boughs are bent with thickset fruit;
My heart is like a rainbow shell
   That paddles in a halcyon sea;
My heart is gladder than all these
   Because my love is come to me.

Raise me a dais of silk and down;
   Hang it with vair and purple dyes;
Carve it in doves and pomegranates;
   And peacocks with a hundred eyes;
Work it in gold and silver grapes,
   In leaves and silver fleurs-de-lys;
Because the birthday of my life
   Is come, my love is come to me.

— CHRISTINA ROSSETTI

A White Rose

The red rose whispers of passion,
    And the white rose breathes of love;
Oh, the red rose is a falcon,
    And the white rose is a dove.

But I send you a cream-white rosebud,
    With a flush on its petal tips;
For the love that is purest and sweetest
    Has a kiss of desire on the lips.

— JOHN BOYLE O'REILLY

Love's Philosophy

The fountains mingle with the river,
    And the rivers with the ocean;
The winds of heaven mix forever,
    With a sweet emotion;
Nothing in the world is single;
    All things by a law divine
In one another's being mingle:—
    Why not I with thine?

See! the mountains kiss high heaven,
    And the waves clasp one another;
No sister flower would be forgiven
    If it disdained its brother;
And the sunlight clasps the earth,
    And the moonbeams kiss the sea:—
What are all these kissings worth,
    If thou kiss not me?

— PERCY BYSSHE SHELLEY

My Ghostly Father,
I Me Confess

My ghostly father, I me confess,
First to God and then to you,
That at a window (wot ye how)
I stole a kiss of great sweetness,
Which done was out advisedness,
But it is done, not undone, now,
My ghostly father, I me confess,
First to God and then to you.
But I restore it shall doubtless
Again, if so be that I mow,
And that, God, I make a vow,
And else I ask forgiveness—
My ghostly father, I me confess,
First to God and then to you.

— CHARLES D'ORLEANS

from **Romeo and Juliet**

ROMEO If I profane with my unworthiest hand
     This holy shrine, the gentle sin is this;
     My lips, two blushing pilgrims, ready
       stand
     To smooth that rough touch with a
       tender kiss.

JULIET Good pilgrim, you do wrong your hand
      too much,
     Which mannerly devotion shows in
      this;
     For saints have hands that pilgrims'
      hands do touch,
     And palm to palm is holy palmers' kiss.

ROMEO Have not saints lips, and holy
      palmers too?

JULIET Ay, pilgrim, lips that they must use in
      prayer.

ROMEO   O! then, dear saint, let lips do what
        hands do;
        They pray, Grant thou, lest faith turn
        to despair.
JULIET Saints do not move, though grant for
        prayers' sake.
ROMEO   Then move not, while my prayers'
        effect I take.

— WILLIAM SHAKESPEARE

17

To Dianeme

Give me one kiss,
   And no more;
If so be, this
   Makes you poor,
To enrich you
   I'll restore
For that one, two
   Thousand score.

— ROBERT HERRICK

A Valentine

What shall I send my sweet today,
   When all the woods attune in love?
   And I would show the lark and dove,
That I can love as well as they.

I'll send a locket full of hair,—
   But no, for it might chance to lie
   Too near her heart, and I should die
Of love's sweet envy to be there.

A violet is sweet to give,—
   Ah, stay! she'd touch it with her lips,
   And, after such complete eclipse,
How could my soul consent to live?

I'll send a kiss, for that would be
   The quickest sent, the lightest borne,
   And well I know tomorrow morn
She'll send it back again to me.

Go, happy winds; ah, do not stay,
   Enamoured of my lady's cheek,
   But hasten home, and I'll bespeak
Your services another day!

— Mathilda Betham-Edwards

"First time he kissed me"

First time he kissed me, he but only kiss'd
    The fingers of this hand wherewith I write;
    And ever since, it grew more clean and white,
Slow to world-greetings, quick with its "Oh, list,"
When the angels speak. A ring of amethyst
    I could not wear here, plainer to my sight,
    Than that first kiss. The second pass'd in
      height
The first, and sought the forehead, and
      half miss'd,
Half falling on the hair. Oh, beyond meed!
    That was the chrism of love, which love's
      own crown,
With sanctifying sweetness, did precede.
    The third upon my lips was folded down
In perfect, purple state; since when, indeed,
    I have been proud, and said, "My love,
      my own!"

— ELIZABETH BARRETT BROWNING

An Hour with Thee

An hour with thee! When earliest day
Dapples with gold the eastern grey,
Oh, what can frame my mind to bear
The toil and tumoil, cark and care,
New griefs, which coming hours unfold,
And sad remembrance of the old?
  One hour with thee.

One hour with thee! When burning June
Waves his red flag at pitch of noon;
What shall repay the faithful swain,
His labour on the sultry plain;
And, more than cave or sheltering bough,
Cool feverish blood and throbbing brow?
  One hour with thee.

One hour with thee! When sun is set,
Oh, what can teach me to forget
The thankless labours of the day;
The hopes, the wishes, flung away;
The increasing wants, and lessening gains,
The master's pride, who scorns my pains?
  One hour with thee.

— Sir Walter Scott

Meet Me
in the Green Glen

Love, meet me in the green glen,
    Beside the tall elm-tree,
Where the sweetbriar smells so sweet agen;
    There come with me.
        Meet me in the green glen.

Meet me at the sunset
    Down in the green glen,
Where we've often met
    By hawthorn-tree and foxes' den,
        Meet me in the green glen.

Meet me in the green glen,
    By sweetbriar bushes there;
Meet me by your own sen,
    Where the wild thyme blossoms fair.
        Meet me in the green glen.

Meet me by the sweetbriar,
  By the mole-hill swelling there;
When the west glows like a fire
  God's crimson bed is there.
    Meet me in the green glen.

— John Clare

On a Girdle

That which her slender waist confin'd,
Shall now my joyful temples bind;
No monarch but would give his crown,
His arms might do what this has done.

It was my heavens's extremest sphere,
The pale which held that lovely deer,
My joy, my grief, my hope, my love,
Did all within this circle move.

A narrow compass, and yet there
Dwelt all that good, and all that's fair;
Give me but what this ribbon bound,
Take all the rest the sun goes 'round.

— EDMUND WALLER

"Those lips that Love's own hand did make"

Those lips that Love's own hand did make
Breath'd forth the sound that said "I hate"
To me that languish'd for her sake;
But when she saw my woeful state,
Straight in her heart did mercy come,
Chiding that tongue that, ever sweet,
Was us'd in giving gentle doom,
And taught it thus anew to greet:
"I hate" she alter'd with an end
That follow'd it as gentle day
Doth follow night, who like a fiend
From heaven to hell is flown away:
  "I hate" from hate away she threw,
  And sav'd my life, saying "not you."

— WILLIAM SHAKESPEARE

The First Day

I wish I could remember the first day,
First hour, first moment of your meeting me;
If bright or dim the season, it might be
Summer or winter for aught I can say.
So unrecorded did it slip away,
So blind was I to see and to foresee,
So dull to mark the budding of my tree
That would not blossom yet for many a May.
If only I could recollect it! Such
A day of days! I let it come and go
As traceless as a thaw of bygone snow.
It seemed to mean so little, meant so much!
If only now I could recall that touch,
First touch of hand in hand!—Did one but know!

— CHRISTINA ROSSETTI

if everything happens
that can't be done

if everything happens that can't be done
(and anything's righter
than books
could plan)
the stupidest teacher will almost guess
(with a run
skip
around we go yes)
there's nothing as something as one

one hasn't a why or because or although
(and buds know better
than books
don't grow)
one's anything old being everything new
(with a what
which
around we come who)
one's everyanything so

so world is a leaf so tree is a bough
(and birds sing sweeter
than books
tell how)

so here is away and so your is a my
(with a down
up
around again fly)
forever was never till now

now i love you and you love me
(and books are shuter
than books
can be)
and deep in the high that does nothing but fall
(with a shout
each
around we go all)
there's somebody calling who's we

we're anything brighter than even the sun
(we're everything greater
than books
might mean)
we're everyanything more than believe
(with a spin
leap
alive we're alive)
we're wonderful one times one

— e.e. cummings

28

Admiring
Love

My Beautiful Lady

I love my lady; she is very fair;
Her brow is white, and bound by simple hair;
    Her spirit sits aloof, and high,
    Altho' it looks thro' her soft eye
    Sweetly and tenderly.

As a young forest, when the wind drives thro',
My life is stirred when she breaks on my view.
    Altho' her beauty has such power,
    Her soul is like the simple flower
    Trembling beneath a shower.

As bliss of saints, when dreaming of large wings,
The bloom around her fancied presence flings,
    I feast and wile her absence, by
    Pressing her choice hand passionately—
    Imagining her sigh.

My lady's voice, altho' so very mild,
Maketh me feel as strong wine would a child;
 My lady's touch, however slight,
 Moves all my senses with its might,
 Like to a sudden fright.

A hawk poised high in air, whose nerved wing-tips
Tremble with might suppressed, before he dips,—
 In vigilance, not more intense
 Than I; when her word's gentle sense
 Makes full-eyed my suspense.

Her mention of a thing—august or poor,
Makes it seem nobler than it was before:
 As where the sun strikes, life will gush,
 And what is pale receive a flush,
 Rich hues—a richer blush.

   — THOMAS WOOLNER

She Walks in Beauty

She walks in beauty, like the night
Of cloudless climes and starry skies;
And all that's best of dark and bright
Meet in her aspect and her eyes;
Thus mellow'd to that tender light
Which heaven to gaudy day denies.

One shade the more, one ray the less,
Had half impair'd the nameless grace
Which waves in every raven tress,
Or softly lightens o'er her face;
Where thoughts serenely sweet express
How pure, how dear their dwelling-place.

And on that cheek, and o'er that brow,
So soft, so calm, yet eloquent,
The smiles that win, the tints that glow,
But tell of days in goodness spent,
A mind at peace with all below,
A heart whose love is innocent!

— GEORGE GORDON,
LORD BYRON

Harlem Sweeties

Have you dug the spill
Of Sugar Hill?
Cast your gims
On this sepia thrill:
Brown sugar lassie,
Caramel treat,
Honey-gold baby
Sweet enough to eat.
Peach-skinned girlie,
Coffee and cream,
Chocolate darling
Out of a dream.
Walnut tinted
Or cocoa brown,
Pomegranate-liped
Pride of the town.
Rich cream-colored
To plum-tinted black,
Feminine sweetness
In Harlem's no lack.
Glow of the quince
To blush of the rose.

Persimmon bronze
To cinnamon toes.
Blackberry cordial,
Virginia Dare wine—
All those sweet colors
Flavor Harlem of mine!
Walnut or cocoa,
Let me repeat:
Caramel, brown sugar,
A chocolate treat.
Molasses taffy,
Coffee and cream,
Licorice, clove, cinnamon
To a honey-brown dream.
Ginger, wine-gold,
Persimmon, blackberry,
All through the spectrum
Harlem girls vary—
So if you want to know beauty's
Rainbow-sweet thrill,
Stroll down luscious,
Delicious, *fine* Sugar Hill.

— LANGSTON HUGHES

Cherry-Ripe

There is a garden in her face
  Where roses and white lilies blow;
A heavenly paradise is that place,
  Wherein all pleasant fruits do flow:
    There cherries grow which none may buy
    Till 'Cherry-ripe' themselves do cry.

Those cherries fairly do enclose
  Of orient pearls a double row,
Which when her lovely laughter shows,
  They look like rose-buds filled with snow;
    Yet them nor peer nor prince can buy
    Till 'Cherry-ripe' themselves do cry.

Her eyes like angels watch them still;
  Her brows like bended bows do stand,
Threatening with piercing frowns to kill
  All that attempt with eye or hand
    Those sacred cherries to come nigh,
    Till 'Cherry-ripe' themselves do cry.

— THOMAS CAMPION

36

A Song: When June Is Past, the Fading Rose

Ask me no more where Jove bestows,
When June is past, the fading rose;
For in your beauty's orient deep
These flowers as in their causes, sleep.

Ask me no more whither doth stray
The golden atoms of the day;
For in pure love heaven did prepare
Those powders to enrich your hair.

Ask me no more whither doth haste
The nightingale, when May is past;
For in your sweet dividing throat
She winters and keeps warm her note.

Ask me no more where those stars' light
That downwards fall in dead of night;
For in your eyes they sit, and there,
Fixèd become, as in their sphere.

Ask me no more if east or west
The phoenix builds her spicy nest;
For unto you at last she flies,
And in your fragrant bosom dies.

— THOMAS CAREW

"What guile is this, that those her golden tresses"

What guile is this, that those her golden tresses,
She doth attire under a net of gold;
And with sly skill so cunningly them dresses,
That which is gold or hair, may scarce be told?
Is it that men's frail eyes, which gaze too bold,
She may entangle in that golden snare;
And being caught may craftily enfold,
Their weaker hearts, which are not well aware?
Take heed therefore, mine eyes, how ye do stare
Henceforth too rashly on that guileful net,
In which if ever ye entrappèd are,
Out of her bands ye by no means shall get.
Fondness it were for any being free,
To covet fetters, though they golden be.

— EDMUND SPENSER

"She was a Phantom of delight"

She was a Phantom of delight
When first she gleamed upon my sight;
A lovely Apparition, sent
To be a moment's ornament;
Her eyes as stars of Twilight fair;
Like Twilight's, too, her dusky hair;
But all things else about her drawn
From May-time and the cheerful Dawn;
A dancing Shape, an Image gay,
To haunt, to startle, and way-lay.

I saw her upon nearer view,
A Spirit, yet a Woman too!
Her household motions light and free,
And steps of virgin-liberty;
A countenance in which did meet
Sweet records, promises as sweet;
A Creature not too bright or good
For human nature's daily food;
For transient sorrows, simple wiles,
Praise, blame, love, kisses, tears, and smiles.

And now I see with eye serene
The very pulse of the machine;
A Being breathing thoughtful breath,
A Traveller between life and death;
The reason firm, the temperate will,
Endurance, foresight, strength, and
  skill;
A perfect Woman, nobly planned,
To warn, to comfort, and command;
And yet a Spirit still, and bright
With something of angelic light.

— WILLIAM WORDSWORTH

To Helen

Helen, thy beauty is to me
   Like those Nicèan barks of yore,
That gently, o'er a perfumed sea,
   The weary, way-worn wanderer bore
   To his own native shore.

On desperate seas long wont to roam,
   Thy hyacinth hair, thy classic face,
Thy Naiad airs have brought me home
   To the glory that was Greece
And the grandeur that was Rome.

Lo! In yon brilliant window-niche
   How statue-like I see thee stand,
   The agate lamp within thy hand!
Ah, Psyche, from the regions which
   Are Holy Land!

— EDGAR ALLAN POE

Upon Julia's Clothes

Whenas in silks my Julia goes,
Then, then, methinks, how sweetly flows
That liquefaction of her clothes.

Next, when I cast mine eyes and see
That brave vibration each way free,
O how that glittering taketh me!

— ROBERT HERRICK

To Citriodora

I turn and see you passing in the street
When you are not. I take another way,
Lest missing you the fragrance of the day
Exhale, and I know not that it is sweet.
And marking you I follow, and when we meet
Love laughs to see how sudden I am gay;
Sweetens the air with fragrance like a spray
Of sweet verbena, and bids my heart to beat.

Love laughs; and girls that take you by the hand,
Know that a sweet thing has befallen them;
And women give their hearts into your heart.
There is, I think, no man in all the land
But would be glad to touch your garment's hem.
And I, I love you with a love apart.

— PHILIP HENRY SAVAGE

44

To a Dark Girl

I love you for your browness,
And the rounded darkness of your breast,
I love you for the breaking sadness in your voice
And shadows where your wayward eyelids rest.

Something of old forgotten queens
Lurks in the lithe abandon of your walk
And something of the shackled slave
Sobs in the rhythm of your talk.

Oh, little brown girl, born for sorrow's mate,
Keep all you have of queenliness,
Forgetting that you once were slave,
And let your full lips laugh at Fate!

— GWENDOLYN BENNETT

Love Song

She is a reed swaying in blue;
Chokecherries are the color of her
skin and her feet moisten the earth.
She sings and prays for the ochre moon
like the first woman.

— EARLE THOMPSON

Annie Laurie

Maxwelton's braes are bonnie
Where early fa's the dew,
And it's there that Annie Laurie
Gie'd me her promise true;
Gie'd me her promise true,
Which ne'er forgot will be;
And for bonnie Annie Laurie
I'd lay me doun and dee.

Her brow is like the snaw drift;
Her throat is like the swan;
Her face it is the fairest
The e'er the sun shone on—
The e'er the sun shone on—
And dark blue is her ee;
And for bonnie Annie Laurie
I'd lay me doun and dee.

Like dew on the gowan lying
Is the fa' o' her fairy feet;
And like the winds in summer sighing,
Her voice is low and sweet—
Her voice is low and sweet—
And she's s' the world to me;
And for bonnie Annie Laurie
I'd lay me doun and dee.

— WILLIAM DOUGLAS

A Red, Red Rose

O my luve is like a red, red rose,
  That's newly sprung in June.
O my luve is like the melodie
  That's sweetly played in tune.

As fair art thou, my bonnie lass,
  So deep in luve am I;
And I will luve thee still, my dear,
  Till a' the seas gang dry.

Till a' the seas gang dry, my dear,
  And the rocks melt wi' the sun!
And I will love thee still, my dear.
  While the sands o' life shall run.

And fare thee weel, my only luve,
  And fare thee weel awhile!
And I will come again, my luve,
  Though it were ten thousand mile!

— ROBERT BURNS

"Shall I compare thee to a summer's day?"

Shall I compare thee to a summer's day?
Thou art more lovely and more temperate:
Rough winds do shake the darling buds of May;
And summer's lease hath all too short a date.
Sometime too hot the eye of heaven shines,
And often is his gold complexion dimm'd;
And every fair from fair sometime declines,
By chance, or nature's changing course
 untrimm'd;
But thy eternal summer shall not fade,
Nor lose possession of that fair thou owest;
Nor shall Death brag thou wand'rest in his shade,
When in eternal lines to time thou growest:
 So long as men can breathe, or eyes can see,
 So long lives this, and this gives life to thee.

— WILLIAM SHAKESPEARE

Sonnet

When midst the summer-roses the warm bees
   Are swarming in the sun, and thou—so full
   Of innocent glee—dost with thy white hands
     pull
Pink scented apples from the garden trees
To fling at me, I catch them, on my knees,
   Like those who gather'd manna; and I cull
   Some hasty buds to pelt thee—white as wool
Lilies, or yellow jonquils, or heartsease;—
Then I can speak my love, e'vn tho' thy smiles
   Gush out among thy blushes, like a flock
Of bright birds from rose-bowers; but when
    thou'rt gone
I have no speech,—no magic that beguiles,
   The stream of utterance from the harden'd
    rock:—
The dial cannot speak without the sun!

— (Major Robert) Calder Campbell

51

A Praise of His Love

Give place, ye lovers, here before
That spent your boasts and brags it vain;
My lady's beauty passeth more
The best of yours, I dare well sayn,
Than doth the sun the candle-light,
Or brightest day the darkest night.

And thereto hath a troth as just
As had Penelope the fair;
For what she saith, ye may it trust,
As it by writing sealèd were;
And virtues hath she many mo
Than I with pen have skill to show.

I could rehearse, if that I wold,
The whole effect of Nature's plaint,
When she had lost the perfit mould,
The like to whom she could not paint;
With wringing hands, how she did cry,
And what she said, I know it, I.

I know she swore with raging mind,
Her kingdom only set apart,
There was no loss by law of kind,
That could have gone so near her heart;
And this was chiefly all her pain;
She could not make the like again.

Sith Nature thus gave her the praise,
To be the chiefest work she wrought;
In faith, methink, some better ways
On your behalf might well be sought,
Than to compare, as ye have done,
To match the candle with the sun.

— HENRY HOWARD, EARL OF SURREY

"My mistress' eyes are nothing like the sun"

My mistress' eyes are nothing like the sun;
Coral is far more red than her lips' red:
If snow be white, why then her breasts are dun;
If hairs be wires, black wires grow on her head.
I have seen roses damasked, red and white,
But no such roses see I in her cheeks;
And in some perfumes is there more delight
Than in the breath that from my mistress reeks.
I love to hear her speak, yet well I know
That music hath a far more pleasing sound:
I grant I never saw a goddess go,—
My mistress, when she walks, treads on the
 ground.
   And yet, by heaven, I think my love as rare
   As any she belied with false compare.

— WILLIAM SHAKESPEARE

Stella's Birthday

Stella, this day is thirty-four
(We shan't dispute a year or more);
However, Stella, be not troubled,
Although thy size and years are doubled
Since first I saw thee at sixteen,
The brightest virgin on the green.
So little is thy form declined,
Made up so largely in thy mind.

Oh! would it please the gods to split
Thy beauty, size, and years, and wit,
No age could furnish out a pair
Of nymphs so graceful, wise, and fair,
With half the lustre of your eyes,
With half your wit, your years, and size.
And then, before it grew too late,
How should I beg of gentle Fate
(That either nymph might have her swain)
To split my worship too in twain.

— JONATHAN SWIFT

Love Poem

My clumsiest dear, whose hands shipwreck vases,
At whose quick touch all glasses chip and ring,
Whose palms are bulls in china, burs in linen,
And have no cunning with any soft thing

Except all ill-at-ease fidgeting people:
The refugee uncertain at the door
You make at home; deftly you steady
The drunk clambering on his undulant floor.

Unpredictable dear, the taxi drivers' terror,
Shrinking from far headlights pale as a dime
Yet leaping before red apoplectic streetcars—
Misfit in any space. And never on time.

A wrench in clocks and the solar system. Only
With words and people and love you move
    at ease.
In traffic of wit expertly manoeuvre
And keep us, all devotion, at your knees.

Forgetting your coffee spreading on our flannel,
Your lipstick grinning on our coat,
So gayly in love's unbreakable heaven
Our souls on glory of spilt bourbon float.

Be with me, darling, early and late. Smash
    glasses—
I will study wry music for your sake.
For should your hands drop white and empty
All the toys of the world would break.

— JOHN FREDERICK NIMS

I Saw My Lady Weep

I saw my Lady weep,
And Sorrow proud to be advanced so
In those fair eyes, where all perfections keep;
   Her face was full of woe,
But such a woe (believe me) as wins more hearts
Than mirth can do, with her enticing parts.

Sorrow was there made fair,
And Passion, wise; Tears, a delightful thing;
Silence, beyond all speech, a wisdom rare;
   She made her sighs to sing,
And all things with so sweet a sadness move;
As made my heart both grieve and love.

O Fairer than aught else
The world can shew, leave off, in time, to grieve,
Enough, enough! Your joyful look excels;
   Tears kill the heart, believe,
O strive not to be excellent in woe,
Which only breeds your beauty's overthrow.

— ANONYMOUS

"Not marble, nor the gilded monuments"

Not marble, nor the gilded monuments
Of princes, shall outlive this powerful rhyme;
But you shall shine more bright in these contents
Than unswept stone, besmear'd with sluttish
  time.
When wasteful war shall statues overturn,
And broils root out the work of masonry,
Nor Mars his sword nor war's quick fire shall
  burn
The living record of your memory.
'Gainst death and all-oblivious enmity
Shall you pace forth; your praise shall still find
  room
Even in the eyes of all posterity
That wear this world out to the ending doom.
  So, till the judgment that yourself arise,
  You live in this, and dwell in lovers' eyes.

— WILLIAM SHAKESPEARE

Deepening
Love

"This heart is not"

This heart is not
a summer field,
and yet . . .
how dense love's foliage
has grown.

— IZUMI SHIKIBU

from **Rubaiyat**

A Book of Verses underneath the Bough,
A Jug of Wine, a Loaf of Bread—and Thou
   Beside me singing in the Wilderness—
Oh, Wilderness were Paradise enow!

— OMAR KHAYYÁM

Meeting at Night

I

The grey sea and the long black land;
And the yellow half-moon large and low;
And the startled little waves that leap
In fiery ringlets from their sleep,
As I gain the cove with pushing prow,
And quench its speed i' the slushy sand.

II

Then a mile of warm sea-scented beach;
Three fields to cross till a farm appears;
A tap at the pane, the quick sharp scratch
And blue spurt of a lighted match,
And a voice less loud, thro' its joys and fears,
Than the two hearts beating each to each!

— ROBERT BROWNING

I Lived with Visions

I lived with visions for my company,
Instead of men and women, years ago,
And found them gentle mates,
 nor thought to know
A sweeter music than they played to me.
But soon their trailing purple was not free
Of this world's dust,—their lutes did silent grow,
And I myself grew faint and blind below
Their vanishing eyes. Then THOU didst come . . .
 to be,
Belovèd, what they seemed. Their shining fronts,
Their songs, their splendours, (better, yet
 the same,
As river-water hallowed into fonts)
Met in thee, and from out thee overcame
My soul with satisfaction of all wants—
Because God's gifts put man's best dreams
 to shame.

— ELIZABETH BARRETT BROWNING

The Good Morrow

I wonder by my troth, what thou and I
  Did, till we loved? Were we not weaned till
    then?
But sucked on country pleasures, childishly?
  Or snorted we i'the seven sleepers' den?
'Twas so; But this, all pleasures fancies be.
If ever any beauty I did see,
Which I desired, and got, 'twas but a dream of
    thee.

And now good morrow to our waking souls,
  Which watch not one another out of fear;
For love, all love of other sights controls,
  And makes one little room, an everywhere.
Let sea-discoverers to new worlds have gone,
Let maps to others, worlds on worlds have
    shown,
Let us possess our world, each hath one, and is
    one.

My face in thine eye, thine in mine appears,
  And true plain hearts do in the faces rest,
Where can we find two better hemispheres
  Without sharp North, without declining West?
Whatever dies, was not mixed equally;
  If our two loves be one, or, thou and I
Love so alike, that none do slacken, none can die.

— JOHN DONNE

Love Song

My love, we will go, we will go, I and you,
And away in the woods we will scatter the dew;
And the salmon behold, and the ousel too,
My love, I and you, we will hear, we will hear,
The calling afar of the doe and the deer,
And the bird in the branches will cry for us clear,
And the cuckoo unseen in his festival mood;
And death, oh my fair one, will never come near
In the bosom afar of the fragrant wood.

— W. B. YEATS

A Sonnet of the Moon

Look how the pale queen of the silent night
Doth cause the ocean to attend upon her,
And he, as long as she is in his sight,
With her full tide is ready her to honor.
But when the silver waggon of the moon
Is mounted up so high he cannot follow,
The sea calls home his crystal waves to moan,
And with low ebb doth manifest his sorrow.
So you that are the sovereign of my heart
Have all my joys attending on your will;
My joys low-ebbing when you do depart,
When you return their tide my heart doth fill.
So as you come and as you do depart,
Joys ebb and flow within my tender heart.

— CHARLES BEST

"Some glory in their birth, some in their skill"

Some glory in their birth, some in their skill,
Some in their wealth, some in their body's force,
Some in their garments, though new-fangled ill,
Some in their hawks and hounds, some in
  their horse;
And every humor hath his adjunct pleasure,
Wherein it finds a joy above the rest,
But these particulars are not my measure,
All these I better in one general best.
Thy love is [better] than high birth to me,
Richer than wealth, prouder than garments' cost,
Of more delight than hawks or horses be;
And having thee, of all men's pride I boast:
    Wretched in this alone, that thou mayst take
    All this away, and me most wretched make.

— WILLIAM SHAKESPEARE

Song

How many times do I love thee, dear?
　　Tell me how many thoughts there be
　　　　In the atmosphere
　　　　Of a new-fall'n year,
Whose white and sable hours appear
　　The latest flake of Eternity:—
So many times do I love thee, dear.

How many times do I love again?
　　Tell me how many beads there are
　　　　In a silver chain
　　　　Of evening rain,
Unravelled from the tumbling main,
　　And threading the eye of a yellow star:—
So many times do I love again.

— THOMAS LOVELL BEDDOES

"How do I love thee?
Let me count the ways"

How do I love thee? Let me count the ways.
I love thee to the depth and breadth and height
My soul can reach, when feeling out of sight
For the ends of Being and ideal Grace.
I love thee to the level of every day's
Most quiet need, by sun and candle-light.
I love thee freely, as men strive for Right;
I love thee purely, as they turn from Praise.
I love thee with the passion put to use
In my old griefs, and with my childhood's faith.
I love thee with a love I seemed to lose
With my lost saints—I love thee with the breath,
Smiles, tears, of all my life!—and, if God choose,
I shall but love thee better after death.

— ELIZABETH BARRET BROWNING

Love

I love you,
Not only for what you are,
But for what I am
When I am with you.

I love you,
Not only for what
You have made of yourself,
But for what
You are making of me.

I love you
For the part of me
That you bring out;
I love you
For putting your hand

Into my heaped-up heart
And passing over
All the foolish, weak things
That you can't help
Dimly seeing there,
And for drawing out
Into the light
All the beautiful belongings
That no one else had looked
Quite far enough to find.

I love you because you
Are helping me to make
Of the lumber of my life
Not a tavern
But a temple;
Out of the works
Of my every day
Not a reproach
But a song.

I love you
Because you have done
More than any creed
Could have done
To make me good,
And more than any fate
Could have done
To make me happy.

You have done it
Without a touch,
Without a word,
Without a sign.
You have done it
By being yourself.
Perhaps that is what
Being a friend means,
After all.

— ROY CROFT

When, Dearest, I But Think On Thee

When, dearest, I but think on thee,
Methinks all things that lovely be
Are present, and my soul delighted:
  For beauties that from worth arise
  Are like the grace of deities,
Still present with us, though unsighted.

Thus while I sit and sigh the day
With all his spreading lights away,
Till night's black wings do overtake me:
  Thinking on thee, thy beauties then,
  As sudden lights do sleeping men,
So they by their bright rays awake me.

Thus absence dies, and dying proves
No absence can consist with loves
That do partake of fair perfection:
    Since in the darkest night they may
    By their quick motion find a way
To see each other by reflection.

    The waving sea can with such flood
Bathe some high palace that hath stood
Far from the main up in the river:
    Oh think not then but love can do
    As much, for that's an ocean too,
That flows not every day, but ever.

— OWEN FELLTHAM

Her Face

Her face
so fair
first bent
mine eye

Her tongue
so sweet
then drew
mine ear

Her wit
so sharp
then hit
my heart

Mine eye
to like
her face
doth lead

Mine ear
to learn
her tongue
doth teach

My heart
to love
her wit
doth move

Her face
with beams
doth blind
mine eye

Her tongue
with sound
doth charm
mine ear

Her wit
with art
doth knit
my heart

Mine eye
with life
her face
doth feed

Mine ear
with hope
her tongue
doth feast

My heart
with skill
her wit
doth fill

O face
with frowns
wrong not
mine eye

O tongue
with checks
vex not
mine ear

O wit
with smart
wound not
my heart

This eye
shall joy
her face
to serve

This ear
shall yield
her tongue
to trust

This heart
shall swear
her wit
to fear.

— ARTHUR GORGES

If Thou Must Love Me

If thou must love me, let it be for nought
Except for love's sake only. Do not say
"I lover her for her smile . . . her look . . . her way
Of speaking gently, . . . for a trick of thought
That falls in well with mine, and certes brought
A sense of pleasant ease on such a day"—
For these things in themselves, Beloved, may
Be changed, or change for thee,—and love, so
    wrought,
May be unwrought so. Neither love me for
Thine own dear pity's wiping my cheeks dry,
A creature might forget to weep who bore
Thy comfort long, and lose thy love thereby.
But love me for love's sake, that evermore
Thou may'st love on, through love's eternity.

— ELIZABETH BARRET BROWNING

The Thought of Her

My love for thee doth take me unaware,
  When most with lesser things my brain is
  wrought
  As in some nimble interchange of thought
The silence enters, and the talkers stare.
Suddenly I am still and thou art there,
  A viewless visitant and unbesought,
  And all my thinking trembles into nought
And all my being opens like a prayer.
Thou art the lifted Chalice in my soul,
  And I a dim church at the thought of thee;
    Brief be the moment, but the mass is said,
The benediction like an aureole
  Is on my spirit, and shuddering through me
  A rapture like the rapture of the dead.

— RICHARD HOVEY

82

Song

She's somewhere in the sunlight strong,
   Her tears are in the falling rain,
She calls me in the wind's soft song,
   And with the flowers she comes again.

Yon bird is but her messenger,
   The moon is but her silver car;
Yea! Sun and moon are sent by her,
   And every wistful, waiting star.

— RICHARD LE GALLIENNE

"*I will give my love an apple
without e'er a core*"

I will give my love an apple without e'er a core,
I will give my love a house without e'er a door,
I will give my love a palace wherein she may be
And she may unlock it without e'er a key.

My head is the apple without e'er a core,
My mind is the house without e'er a door,
My heart is the palace wherein she may be
And she may unlock it without e'er a key

I will give my love a cherry without e'er a stone,
I will give my love a chick without e'er a bone,
I will give my love a ring, not a rent to be seen,
I will get my love children without any crying.

When the cherry's in blossom there's never no
  stone,
When the chick's in the womb there's never no
  bone,
And when they're rinning running not a rent to be
  seen,
And when they're child-making they're seldom
  crying.

— ANONYMOUS

Love's Calendar

The Summer comes and the Summer goes;
Wild-flowers are fringing the dusty lanes,
The swallows go darting through fragrant rains,
Then, all of a sudden—it snows.

Dear Heart, our lives so happily flow,
So lightly we heed the flying hours,
We only know Winter is gone—by the flowers,
We only know Winter is come—by the snow.

— THOMAS BAILEY ALDRICH

Challenging Love

Invitation to Love

Come when the nights are bright with stars
Or come when the moon is mellow;
Come when the sun his golden bars
Drops on the hay-field yellow.
Come in the twilight soft and gray,
Come in the night or come in the day,
Come, O love, whene'er you may,
And you are welcome, welcome.

You are sweet, O Love, dear Love,
You are soft as the nesting dove.
Come to my heart and bring it to rest
As the bird flies home to its welcome nest.

Come when my heart is full of grief
Or when my heart is merry;
Come with the falling of the leaf
Or with the redd'ning cherry.
Come when the year's first blossom blows,
Come when the summer gleams and glows,
Come with the winter's drifting snows,
And you are welcome, welcome.

— PAUL LAURENCE DUNBAR

89

Love Song

Sweep the house clean,
hang fresh curtains
in the windows
put on a new dress
and come with me!
The elm is scattering
its little loaves
of sweet smells
from a white sky!
Who shall hear of us
in the time to come?
Let him say there was
a burst of fragrance
from black branches.

— WILLIAM CARLOS WILLIAMS

Maud

Come into the garden, Maud,
  For the black bat, Night, has flown,
Come into the garden, Maud,
  I am here at the gate alone;
And the woodbine spices are wafted abroad,
  And the musk of the roses blown.

For a breeze of morning moves,
  And the planet of Love is on high,
Beginning to faint in the light that she loves
  On a bed of daffodil sky,
To faint in the light of the sun she loves,
  To faint in his light, and to die.

All night have the roses heard
  The flute, violin, bassoon;
All night has the casement jessamine stirr'd
  To the dancers dancing in tune;
Till a silence fell with the waking bird,
  And a hush with the setting moon.

I said to the lily, "There is but one
  With whom she has heart to be gay.
When will the dancers leave her alone?
  She is weary of dance and play."
Now half to the setting moon are gone,
  And half to the rising day;

Low on the sand and loud on the stone
    The last wheel echoes away.

I said to the rose, "The brief night goes
    In babble and revel and wine.
O young lord-lover, what sighs are those
    For one that will never be thine?
But mine, but mine," so I sware to the rose,
    "For ever and ever, mine."

And the soul of the rose went into my blood,
    As the music clash'd in the hall;
And long by the garden lake I stood,
    For I heard your rivulet fall
From the lake to the meadow and on to the wood,
    Our wood, that is dearer than all;

From the meadow your walks have left so sweet
    That whenever a March-wind sighs
He sets the jewel-print of your feet
    In violets blue as your eyes,
To the woody hollows in which we meet
    And the valleys of Paradise.

The slender acacia would not shake
    One long milk-bloom on the tree;
The white lake-blossom fell into the lake,
    As the pimpernel dozed on the lea;
But the rose was awake all night for your sake,
    Knowing your promise to me;

The lilies and roses were all awake,
  They sigh'd for the dawn and thee.

Queen rose of the rosebud garden of girls,
  Come hither, the dances are done,
In gloss of satin and glimmer of pearls,
  Queen lily and rose in one;
Shine out, little head, sunning over with curls.
  To the flowers, and be their sun.

There has fallen a splendid tear
  From the passion-flower at the gate.
She is coming, my dove, my dear;
  She is coming, my life, my fate;
The red rose cries, "She is near, she is near";
  And the white rose weeps, "She is late";
The larkspur listens, "I hear, I hear";
  And the lily whispers, "I wait."

She is coming, my own, my sweet;
  Were it ever so airy a tread,
My heart would hear her and beat,
  Were it earth in an earthy bed;
My dust would hear her and beat,
  Had I lain for a century dead;
Would start and tremble under her feet,
  And blossom in purple and red.

— ALFRED, LORD TENNYSON

93

Love's Springtide

My heart was winter-bound until
   I heard you sing;
O voice of Love, hush not, but fill
   My life with Spring!

My hopes were homeless things before
   I saw your eyes;
O smile of Love, close not the door
   To paradise!

My dreams were bitter once, and then
   I found them bliss;
O lips of Love, give me again
   Your rose to kiss!

Springtide of Love! The secret sweet
   Is ours alone;
O heart of Love, at last you beat
   Against my own!

— FRANK DEMPSTER SHERMAN

94

Summer

Come we to the summer, to the summer we will
  come,
For the woods are full of bluebells and the hedges
  full of bloom,
And the crow is on the oak a-building of her nest,
And love is burning diamonds in my true lover's
  breast;
She sits beneath the whitehorn a-plaiting of her
  hair,
And I will to my true lover with a fond request
  repair;
I will look upon her face, I will in her beauty rest,
And lay my aching weariness upon her lovely
  breast.

The clock-a-clay is creeping on the open bloom of
  May
The merry bee is trampling the pinky threads all
  day,
And the chaffinch it is brooding on its grey mossy
  nest
In the whitehorn bush where I will lean upon my
  lover's breast;
I'll lean upon her breast and I'll whisper in her ear
That I cannot get a wink o'sleep for thinking of
  my dear;
I hunger at my meat and I daily fade away
Like the hedge rose that is broken in the heat of
  the day.

— JOHN CLARE

You'll Love Me Yet

You'll love me yet!—and I can tarry
   Your love's protracted growing:
June rear'd that bunch of flowers you carry,
   From seeds of April's sowing.

I plant a heartful now: some seed
   At least is sure to strike,
And yield—what you'll not pluck indeed,
   Not love, but, may be, like.

You'll look at least on love's remains,
   A grave 's one violet:
Your look?—that pays a thousand pains.
   What 's death? You'll love me yet!

— ROBERT BROWNING

The Passionate Shepherd
to His Love

Come live with me and be my love,
And we will all the pleasures prove
That valleys, groves, hills, and fields,
Woods, or steepy mountain yields.

And we will sit upon the rocks
Seeing the shepherds feed their flocks,
By shallow rivers, to whose falls
Melodious birds sing madrigals.

And I will make thee beds of roses
And a thousand fragrant posies,
A cap of flowers and a kirtle
Embroider'd all with leaves of myrtle.

A gown made of the finest wool,
Which from our pretty lambs we pull;
Fair linèd slippers for the cold,
With buckles of the purest gold.

A belt of straw and ivy buds,
With coral clasps and amber studs:
And if these pleasures may thee move,
Come live with me and be my love.

The shepherd swains shall dance and sing
For thy delight each May morning:
If these delights thy mind may move,
Then live with me and be my love.

— CHRISTOPHER MARLOWE

The Nymph's Reply
to the Shepherd

If all the world and love were young,
And truth in every shepherd's tongue,
These pretty pleasures might me move
To live with thee and be thy love.

Time drives the flocks from field to fold,
When rivers rage and rocks grow cold,
And Philomel becometh dumb;
The rest complains of cares to come.

The flowers do fade, and wanton fields
To wayward winter reckoning yields:
A honey tongue, a heart of gall,
Is fancy's spring, but sorrow's fall.

Thy gowns, thy shoes, thy beds of roses,
Thy cap, thy kirtle, and thy posies
Soon break, soon wither, soon forgotten,
In folly ripe, in reason rotten.

Thy belt of straw and ivy buds,
Thy coral clasps and amber studs,
All these in me no means can move
To come to thee and be thy love.

But could youth last and love still breed,
Had joys no date nor age no need,
Then these delights my mind might move
To live with thee and be thy love.

— SIR WALTER RALEIGH

An Answer to Another Persuading a Lady to Marriage

Forbear, bold youth, all's Heaven here,
 And what you do aver,
To others, courtship may appear,
 'Tis sacriledge to her.

She is a publick deity,
 And were't not very odd
She should depose her self to be
 A pretty household god?

First make the sun in private shine,
 And bid the world adieu,
That so he may his beams confine
 In complement to you.

But if of that you do despair,
 Think how you did amiss,
To strive to fix her beams which are
 More bright and large than this.

— KATHERINE PHILIPS

My Dear
and Only Love

My dear and only Love, I pray
　　This noble world of thee
Be govern'd by no other sway
　　But purest monarchy;
For if confusion have a part,
　　Which virtuous souls abhor,
And hold a synod in thy heart,
　　I'll never love thee more.

Like Alexander I will reign,
　　And I will reign alone,
My thoughts shall evermore disdain
　　A rival on my throne.
He either fears his fate too much,
　　Or his deserts are small,
That puts it not unto the touch
　　To win or lose it all.

But I must rule and govern still,
　　And always give the law,
And have each subject at my will,
　　And all to stand in awe.

But 'gainst my battery, if I find
    Thou shunn'st the prize so sore
As thou sett'st me up a blind,
    I'll never love thee more.

Or in the empire of thy heart
    Where I should solely be,
Another do pretend a part
    And dares to vie with me;
Or if committees thou erect,
    And go on such a score,
I'll sing and laugh at thy neglect,
    And never love thee more.

But if thou wilt be constant then,
    And faithful of thy word,
I'll make thee glorious by my pen
    And famous by my sword;
I'll serve thee in such noble ways
    Was never heard before;
I'll crown and deck thee all with bays,
    And love thee evermore.

— JAMES GRAHAM,
MARQUIS OF MONTROSE

Don't Tell the World that You're Waiting for Me

Three summers have gone since the first time we
    met, love,
    And still 'tis in vain that I ask thee to wed;
I hear no reply but a gentle "Not yet, love,"
    With a smile of your lip, and a shake of your
    head.
Ah! how oft have I whispered, how oft have I
    sued thee,
    And breathed my soul's question of "When
    shall it be?"
You know, dear, how long and how truly I've
    wooed thee,
    So don't tell the world that you're waiting for
    me.

I have fashioned a home, where the fairies might
   dwell, love,
   I've planted the myrtle, the rose, and the vine;
But the cottage to me is a mere hermit's cell, love,
   And the bloom will be dull till the flowers are
   thine.
I've a ring of bright gold, which I gaze on when
   lonely,
   And sigh with Hope's eloquence, "When will it
   be?"
There needs but thy "Yes," love—one little word
   only,
   So don't tell the world that you're waiting for
   me.

— ELIZA COOK

Ruth

She stood breast high amid the corn,
Clasped by the golden light of morn,
Like the sweetheart of the sun,
Who many a glowing kiss had won.

On her cheek an autumn flush,
Deeply ripened;—such a blush
In the midst of brown was born,
Like red poppies grown with corn.

Round her eyes her tresses fell,
Which were blackest none could tell,
But long lashes veiled a light,
That had else been all too bright.

And her hat, with shady brim,
Made her tressy forehead dim;—
Thus she stood amid the stooks,
Praising God with sweetest looks:—

Sure , I said, heaven did not mean,
Where I reap thou shouldst but glean,
Lay thy sheaf adown and come,
Share my harvest and my home.

— THOMAS HOOD

To Anthea,
Who May Command
Him Anything

Bid me to live, and I will live
    Thy protestant to be;
Or bid me love, and I will give
    A loving heart to thee.

A heart as soft, a heart as kind,
    A heart as sound and free,
As in the whole world thou canst find,
    That heart I'll give to thee.

Bid that heart stay, and it will stay,
    To honour thy decree;
Or bid it languish quite away,
    And 't shall do so for thee.

Bid me to weep, and I will weep,
   While I have eyes to see;
And having none, yet I will keep
   A heart to weep for thee.

Bid me despair, and I'll despair,
   Under that cypress tree;
Or bid me die, and I will dare
   E'en death, to die for thee.

Thou art my life, my love, my heart,
   The very eyes of me;
And hast command of every part,
   To live and die for thee.

— ROBERT HERRICK

The Indian Serenade

I arise from dreams of thee
In the first sweet sleep of night,
When the winds are breathing low,
And the stars are shining bright
I arise from dreams of thee,
And a spirit in my feet
Hath led me—who knows how?
To thy chamber window, Sweet!

The wandering airs they faint
On the dark, the silent stream—
The champak odors fail
Like sweet thoughts in a dream;
The nightingale's complaint,
It dies upon her heart;
As I must on thine,
Oh, beloved as thou art!

O lift me from the grass!
I die! I faint! I fail!
Let thy love in kisses rain
On my lips and eyelids pale.
My cheek is cold and white, alas!
My heart beats loud and fast;—
Oh! press it to thine own again,
Where it will break at last.

— PERCY BYSSHE SHELLEY

The Love I Bear Thee

And wilt thou have me fashion into speech
The love I bear thee, finding words enough,
And hold the torch out, while the winds are
  rough,
Between our faces, to cast light on each?—
I drop it at they feet. I cannot teach
My hand to hold my spirit so far off
From myself—me—that I should bring thee proof
In words, of love hid in me out of reach.
Nay, let the silence of my womanhood
Commend my woman-love to thy belief,—
Seeing that I stand unwon, however wooed,
And rend the garment of my life, in brief,
By a most dautless, voiceless fortitude,
Lest one touch of this heart convey its grief.

— ELIZABETH BARRETT BROWNING

Leap Before You Look

The sense of danger must not disappear:
The way is certainly both short and steep,
However gradual it looks from here;
Look if you like, but you will have to leap.

Tough-minded men get mushy in their sleep
And break the by-laws any fool can keep;
It is not the convention but the fear
That has a tendency to disappear.

The worried efforts of the busy heap,
The dirt, the imprecision, and the beer
Produce a few smart wisecracks every year;
Laugh if you can, but you will have to leap.

The clothes that are considered right to wear
Will not be either sensible or cheap,
So long as we consent to live like sheep
And never mention those who disappear.

Much can be said for social savoir-faire,
But to rejoice when no one else is there
Is even harder than it is to weep;
No one is watching, but you have to leap.

A solitude ten thousand fathoms deep
Sustains the bed on which we lie, my dear:
Although I love you, you will have to leap;
Our dream of safety has to disappear.

— W. H. AUDEN

The Fair Singer

To make a final conquest of all me,
Love did compose so sweet an enemy,
In whom both beauties to my death agree,
Joining themselves in fatal harmony;
That while she with her eyes my heart does bind,
She with her voice might captivate my mind.

I could have fled from one but singly fair,
My disentangled soul itself might save,
Breaking the curled trammels of her hair.
But how should I avoid to be her slave,
Whose subtle art invisibly can wreath
My fetters of the very air I breathe?

It had been easy fighting in some plain,
Where victory might hang in equal choice,
But all resistance against her is vain,
Who has th'advantage both of eyes and voice,
And all my forces needs must be undone,
She having gained both the wind and sun.

— ANDREW MARVELL

Many in Aftertimes

Vien dietro a me e lascia dir le genti.—DANTE.
Contando i casi della vita nostra.—PETRARCA.

Many in aftertimes will say of you
  "He loved her"—while of me what will they say?
  Not that I loved you more than just in play,
For fashion's sake as idle women do.
Even let them prate; who know what we knew
  Of love and parting in exceeding pain.
  Of parting hopeless here to meet again,
Hopeless on earth, and heaven is out of view.
But by my heart of love laid bare to you.
  My love that you can make not void or vain,
Love that forgoes you but to claim anew
    Beyond this passage of the gate of death,
  I charge you at the Judgement make it plain
    My love of you was life and not a breath.

— CHRISTINA ROSSETTI

*Lifetime
Love*

Reply

I cannot swear with any certainty
That I will always feel as I do now,
Loving you with the same fierce ecstasy,
Needing the same your lips upon my brow.
Nor can I promise stars forever bright,
Or vow green leaves will never turn to gold.
I cannot see beyond this present night
To say what promises the dawn may hold.
And yet, I know my heart must follow you
High up to hilltops, low through vales of tears,
Through golden days and days of sombre hue.
And love will only deepen with the years,
Becoming sun and shadow, wind and rain,
Wine that grows mellow, bread that will sustain.

— Naomi Long Madgett

To Celia

Not, Celia, that I juster am,
   Or better than the rest;
For I would change each hour like them
   Were not my heart at rest.

But I am tied to very thee,
   By every thought I have;
Thy face I only care to see,
   Thy heart I only crave.

All that in woman is ador'd
   In thy dear self I find;
For the whole sex can but afford
   The handsome and the kind.

Why then should I seek farther store
   And still make love anew?
When change itself can give no more,
   'Tis easy to be true.

— SIR CHARLES SEDLEY

The Kiss

Before you kissed me only winds of heaven
Had kissed me, and the tenderness of rain—
Now you have come, how can I care for kisses
Like theirs again?

I sought the sea, she sent her winds to meet me,
They surged about me singing of the south—
I turned my head away to keep still holy
Your kiss upon my mouth.

And swift sweet rains of shining April weather
Found not my lips where living kisses are;
I bowed my head lest they put out my glory
As rain puts out a star.

I am my love's and he is mine forever,
Sealed with a seal and safe forevermore—
Think you that I could let a beggar enter
Where a king stood before?

— SARA TEASDALE

121

To Asra

Are there two things, of all which men possess,
That are so like each other and so near,
As mutual Love seems like to Happiness?
Dear Asra, woman beyond utterance dear!
This Love which ever welling at my heart,
Now in its living fount doth heave and fall,
Now overflowing pours thro' every part
Of all my frame, and fills and changes all,
Like vernal waters springing up through snow,
This Love that seeming great beyond the power
Of growth, yet seemeth ever more to grow,
Could I transmute the whole to one rich Dower
Of Happy Life, and give it all to Thee,
Thy lot, methinks, were Heaven, thy age,
  Eternity!

— SAMUEL TAYLOR COLERIDGE

Monna Inominata, 4

I loved you first: but afterwards your love,
 Outsoaring mine, sang such a loftier song
As drowned the friendly cooings of my dove.
 Which owes the other most? My love was
  long,
 And yours one moment seemed to wax more
  strong;
I loved and guessed at you, you construed me
And loved me for what might or might not be—
 Nay, weights and measures do us both a wrong.
For verily love knows not "mine" or "thine";
With separate "I" and "thou" free love has done,
 For one is both and both are one in love:
Rich love knows nought of "thine that is not
 mine";
 Both have the strength and both the length
  thereof,
Both of us, of the love which makes us one.

— CHRISTINA ROSSETTI

123

Romance

I will make you brooches and toys for your delight
Of bird-song at morning and star-shine at night.
I will make a palace fit for you and me
Of green days in forests and blue days at sea.

I will make my kitchen, and you shall keep your
  room,
Where white flows the river and bright blows the
  broom,
And you shall wash your linen and keep your body
  white
In rainfall at morning and dewfall at night.

And this shall be for music when no one else is
  near,
The fine song for singing, the rare song to hear!
That only I remember, that only you admire,
Of the broad road that stretches and the roadside
  fire.

— ROBERT LOUIS STEVENSON

Air and Angels

Twice or thrice had I lov'd thee,
Before I knew thy face or name;
So in a voice, so in a shapeless flame
Angels affect us oft, and worshipp'd be;
    Still when, to where thou wert, I came,
Some lovely glorious nothing I did see.
    But since my soul, whose child love is,
Takes limbs of flesh, and else could nothing do,
    More subtle than the parent is
Love must not be, but take a body too;
    And therefore what thou wert, and who,
        I bid Love ask, and now
That it assume thy body, I allow,
And fix itself in thy lip, eye, and brow.

Whilst thus to ballast love I thought,
And so more steadily to have gone,
With wares which would sink admiration,
I saw I had love's pinnace overfraught;
    Ev'ry thy hair for love to work upon
Is much too much, some fitter must be sought;
    For, nor in nothing, nor in things
Extreme, and scatt'ring bright, can love inhere;
    Then, as an angel, face, and wings
Of air, not pure as it, yet pure, doth wear,
    So thy love may be my love's sphere;
        Just such disparity
As is 'twixt air and angels' purity,
'Twixt women's love, and men's, will ever be.

— JOHN DONNE

A Letter to Daphnis, April 2nd 1685

This to the Crown, and blessing of my life,
The much lov'd husband, of a happy wife.
To him, whose constant passion found the art
To win a stubborn, and ungrateful heart;
And to the World, by tend'rest proof discovers
They err, who say that husbands can't be lovers.
With such return of passion, as is due,
Daphnis I love, Daphnis my thoughts persue,
Daphnis, my hopes, my joys, are bounded all in
  you:
Ev'n I, for Daphnis, and my promise sake,
What I in women censure, undertake.
But this from love, not vanity, proceeds;
You know who writes; and I who 'tis that reads.
Judge not my passion, by my want of skill,
Many love well, though they express itt ill;
And I your censure cou'd with pleasure bear,
Wou'd you but soon return, and speak itt here.

— ANNE FINCH, COUNTESS OF WINCHILSEA

"So we'll go no more a-roving"

So, we'll go no more a-roving
   So late into the night,
Though the heart be still as loving
   And the moon be still as bright.

For the sword outwears its sheath,
   And the soul wears out the breast,
And the heart must pause to breathe,
   And love itself have rest.

Though the night was made for loving,
   And the day returns too soon,
Yet we'll go no more a-roving
   By the light of the moon.

        — GEORGE GORDON,
        LORD BYRON

"On a fair morning,
as I came by the way"

On a fair morning, as I came by the way,
Met I with a merry maid in the merry month of
  May,
When a sweet love sings his lovely lay,
And every bird upon the bush bechirps it up so
  gay.
With a heave and ho! with a heave and ho!
Thy wife shall be thy master, I trow.
Sing care away, care away, let the world go!
Hey, lustily, all in a row, all in a row,
Sing care away, care away, let the world go!

— THOMAS MORLEY

"Carry her over the water"

Carry her over the water,
   And set her down under the tree,
Where the culvers white all day and all night,
   And the winds from every quarter,
Sing agreeably, agreeably, agreeably of love.

Put a gold ring on her finger,
   And press her close to your heart,
While the fish in the lake their snapshots take,
   And the frog, that sanguine singer,
Sings agreeably, agreeably, agreeably of love.

The streets shall all flock to your marriage,
   The houses turn round to look,
The tables and chairs say suitable prayers,
   And the horses drawing your carriage
Sing agreeably, agreeably, agreeably of love.

— W. H. Auden

130

From This Day Forward

From this day forward,
You shall not walk alone.
My heart will be your shelter,
And my arms will be your home.

— AUTHOR UNKNOWN

"Let me not to the marriage of true minds admit impediments"

Let me not to the marriage of true minds
Admit impediments; love is not love
Which alters when it alteration finds,
Or bends with the remover to remove.
Oh, no, it is an ever fixèd mark
That looks on tempests and is never shaken;
It is the star to every wand'ring bark,
Whose worth's unknown, although his height be
  taken.
Love's not Time's fool, though rosy lips and cheeks
Within his bending sickle's compass come;
Love alters not with his brief hours and weeks,
But bears it out even to the edge of Doom.
    If this be error and upon me proved,
    I never writ, nor no man ever loved.

— WILLIAM SHAKESPEARE

A Black Wedding Song

First Dedicated to
Charles and La Tanya
Allen and Glenda
Haki and Safisha

I

This love is a rich cry over
the deviltries and death
A weapon-song. Keep it strong.

Keep it strong.
Keep it logic and Magic and lightning and Muscle.

Strong hand in strong hand, stride to
the Assault that is promised you (knowing
no armor assaults a pudding or a mush.)

Here is your Wedding Day.
Here is your launch.

Come to your Wedding Song.

II

For you
I wish the kindness that romps or sorrows along.
Or kneels.
I wish you the daily forgiveness of each other.
For war comes in from the World
and puzzles a darling duet—
tangles tongues,
tears hearts, mashes minds;
there will be the need to forgive.

I wish you the jewels of black love.

Come to your Wedding Song.

— GWENDOLYN BROOKS

from **Adam Bede**

What greater thing is there for two human
  souls,
than to feel that they are joined for life—
to strengthen each other in all labor,
to rest on each other in all sorrow,
to minister to each other in all pain,
to be one with each other
in silent unspeakable memories. . .

— GEORGE ELIOT

I Love You

I love you for what you are, but I
  love you
yet more for what you are going to
  be.
I love you not so much for your
  realities
as for your ideals.
I pray for your desires that they may
  be great,
rather than for your satisfactions,
which may be so hazardously little.
You are going forward toward
  something great.
I am on the way with you,
and therefore I love you.

— CARL SANDBURG

Wedding Prayer

Now you will feel no rain,
  For each of you will be shelter to the other.
Now you will feel no cold,
  For each of you will be warmth to the other.
Now there is no more loneliness,
  For each of you will be companion to the other.
Now you are two bodies,
  But there is only one life before you.
Go now to your dwelling place
  To enter into the days of your togetherness
And may your days be good and long upon the
  earth.

— Traditional Apache Prayer

On Marriage *from* The Prophet

You were born together, and together you shall be
   forevermore.
You shall be together when the white wings of
   death scatter your days.
Ay, you shall be together even in the silent
   memory of God.
But let there be spaces in your togetherness,
And let the winds of heavens dance between you.

Love one another, but make not a bond of love:
Let it rather be a moving sea between the shores
   of your souls.
Fill each other's cup but drink not from one cup.
Give one another of your bread but eat not from
   the same loaf.
Sing and dance together and be joyous, but let
   each one of you be alone,
Even as the strings of a lute are alone though they
   quiver with the same music.

Give your hearts, but not into each other's
 keeping.
For only the hand of Life can contain your hearts.
And stand together yet not too near together:
For the pillars of the temple stand apart,
And the oak tree and the cypress grow not in
 each other's shadow.

— KAHLIL GIBRAN

Any Wife or Husband

Let us be guests in one another's house
With deferential "No" and courteous "Yes";
Let us take care to hide our foolish moods
Behind a certain show of cheerfulness.

Let us avoid all sullen silences;
We should find fresh and sprightly things to say;
I must be fearful lest you find me dull,
And you must dread to be me any way.

Let us knock gently at each other's heart,
Glad of a chance to look within—and yet
Let us remember that to force one's way
Is the unpardoned breach of etiquette.

So shall I be hostess—you, the host—
Until all need for entertainment ends;
We shall be lovers when the last door shuts,
But what is better still—we shall be friends.

— CAROL HAYNES

To My Dear
and Loving Husband

If ever two were one, then surely we.
If ever man were loved by wife, then thee;
If ever wife was happy in a man,
Compare with me, ye women, if you can.
I prize thy love more than whole mines of gold,
Or all the riches that the East doth hold.
My love is such that rivers cannot quench,
Nor aught but love from thee give recompense.
Thy love is such I can no way repay;
The heavens reward thee manifold, I pray.
Then while we live, in love let's so persevere,
That when we live no more, we may live ever.

— ANNE BRADSTREET

"When my love swears that she is made of truth"

When my love swears that she is made of truth,
I do believe her, though I know she lies,
That she might think me some untutored youth,
Unlearnèd in the world's false subtleties.
Thus vainly thinking that she thinks me young,
Although she knows my days are past the best,
Simply I credit her false-speaking tongue;
On both sides thus is simple truth supprest.
But wherefore says she not she is unjust?
And wherefore say not I that I am old?
Oh, love's best habit is in seeming trust,
And age in love loves not to have years told:
Therefore I lie with her and she with me,
And in our faults by lies we flattered be.

— WILLIAM SHAKESPEARE

The Years

To-night I close my eyes and see
A strange procession passing me—
The years before I saw your face
Go by me with a wistful grace;
They pass, the sensitive shy years,
As one who strives to dance, half blind with tears.

The years went by and never knew
Tha each one brought me nearer you;
Their path was narrow and apart
And yet it led me to your heart—
Oh sensitive shy years, oh lonely years,
That strove to sing with voices drowned in tears.

— SARA TEASDALE

143

John Anderson My Jo

John Anderson my Jo, John,
   When we were first acquent;
Your locks were like the raven,
   Your bonny brow was brent;
But now your brow is beld, John,
   Your locks are like the snaw;
But blessings on your frosty pow,
   John Anderson my Jo.

John Anderson my Jo, John,
   We clamb the hill the gither;
And mony a canty day, John,
   We've had wi' ane anither:
Now we maun totter down, John,
   And hand in hand we'll go,
And sleep the gither at the foot,
   John Anderson my Jo.

— ROBERT BURNS

*Irreverent
Love*

O Tell Me the Truth
about Love

Some say love's a little boy,
And some say it's a bird,
Some say it makes the world go around,
Some say that's absurd,
And when I asked the man next-door,
Who looked as if he knew,
His wife got very cross indeed,
And said it wouldn't do.

Does it look like a pair of pyjamas,
Or the ham in a temperance hotel?
Does its odour remind one of llamas,
Or has it a comforting smell?
Is it prickly to touch as a hedge is,
Or soft as eiderdown fluff?
Is it sharp or quite smooth at the edges?
O tell me the truth about love.

Our history books refer to it
In cryptic little notes,
It's quite a common topic on
The Transatlantic boats;

I've found the subject mentioned in
Accounts of suicides,
And even seen it scribbled on
The backs of railway guides.

Does it howl like a hungry Alsatian,
Or boom like a military band?
Could one give a first-rate imitation
On a saw or a Steinway Grand?
Is its singing at parties a riot?
Does it only like Classical stuff?
Will it stop when one wants to be quiet?
O tell me the truth about love.

I looked inside the summer-house;
It wasn't over there;
I tried the Thames at Maidenhead,
And Brighton's bracing air.
I don't know what the blackbird sang,
Or what the tulip said;
But it wasn't in the chicken-run,
Or underneath the bed.

Can it pull extraordinary faces?
Is it usually sick on a swing?
Does it spend all its time at the races,
or fiddling with pieces of string?
Has it views of its own about money?
Does it think Patriotism enough?
Are its stories vulgar but funny?
O tell me the truth about love.

When it comes, will it come without warning
Just as I'm picking my nose?
Will it knock on my door in the morning,
Or tread in the bus on my toes?
Will it come like a change in the weather?
Will its greeting be courteous or rough?
Will it alter my life altogether?
O tell me the truth about love.

— W. H. AUDEN

Song

Pan, grant that I may never prove
So great a *Slave* to fall in love,
And to an Unknown *Deity*
Resign my happy Liberty:
I love to see the Amorous *Swains*
 Unto my Scorn their Hearts resign:
With Pride I see the Meads and Plains
 Throng'd all with *Slaves,* and they all mine:
Whilst I the whining Fools despise,
That pay their Homage to my Eyes.

— APHRA BEHN

The *"Je Ne Sais Quois"*

Yes, I'm in love, I feel it now,
    And Celia has undone me;
And yet I'll swear I can't tell how
    The pleasing plague stole on me.

'Tis not her face that love creates,
    For there no Graces revel;
'Tis not her shape, for there the Fates
    Have rather been uncivil.

'Tis not her air, for sure in that,
    There's nothing more than common;
And all her sense is only chat,
    Like any other woman.

Her voice, her touch, might give the alarm—
    'Tis both perhaps, or neither;
In short, 'tis that provoking charm
    Of Celia altogether.

— WILLIAM WHITEHEAD

To One That Asked Me Why I Loved J.G.

Why do I love? go ask the glorious sun
Why every day it round the world doth run:
Ask Thames and Tiber why they ebb and flow:
Ask damask roses why in June they blow:
Ask ice and hail the reason why they're cold:
Decaying beauties, why they will grow old:
They'll tell thee, Fate, that everything doth move,
Inforces them to this, and me to love.
There is no reason for our love or hate,
'Tis irresistible as Death or Fate;
'Tis not his face; I've sense enough to see,
That is not good, though doated on by me:
Nor is't his tongue, that has this conquest won,
For that at least is equalled by my own:

His carriage can to none obliging be,
'Tis rude, affected, full of vanity:
Strangely ill natur'd, peevish and unkind,
Unconstant, false, to jelousy inclin'd:
His temper could not have so great a power,
'Tis mutable, and changes every hour:
Those vigorous years that women so adore
Are past in him: he's twice my age and more;
And yet I love this false, this worthless man,
With all the passion that a woman can;
Doat on his imperfections, though I spy
Nothing to love; I love, and know not why.
Since 'tis decreed in the dark book of Fate,
That I should love, and he should be ingrate.

— EPHELIA

The Kiss

"I saw you take his kiss!" "'Tis true."
  "O, modesty!" "'Twas strictly kept:
He thought me asleep; at least I knew
  He thought I thought he thought I slept."

— COVENTRY PATMORE

As Sweet

It's all because we're so alike—
Twin souls, we two.
We smile at the expression, yes,
And know it's true.

I told the shrink. He gave our love
A different name.
But he can call it what he likes—
It's still the same.

I long to see you, hear your voice,
My narcissistic object-choice.

— WENDY COPE

Wed

For these white arms about my neck—
   For the dainty room, with its ordered grace—
For my snowy linen without a fleck—
   For the tender charm of this uplift face—

For the softened light and the homelike air—
   The low luxurious cannel fire—
The padded ease of my chosen chair—
   The devoted love that discounts desire—

I sometimes think, when Twelve is struck
   By the clock on the mantel, tinkling clear,
I would take—and thank the gods for the luck—
   One single hour with the boys and the beer.

Where the sawdust scent of a cheap saloon
   Is mingled with malt; where each man smokes,
Where they sing the street songs out of tune,
   Talk Art, and bandy ephemeral jokes.

By Jove, I do! And all the time
   I know not a man that is there to-night
But would barter his brains to be where I'm—
   And I'm well aware that the beggars are right.

      — HENRY CUYLER BUNNER

Love

There's the wonderful love of a beautiful maid,
  And the love of a staunch true man,
And the love of a baby that's unafraid—
  All have existed since time began.
But the most wonderful love, the Love of all
  loves,
    Even greater than the love for Mother,
Is the infinite, tenderest, passionate love
  Of one dead drunk for another.

— ANONYMOUS

One Perfect Rose

A single flow'r he sent me, since we met.
   All tenderly his messenger he chose;
Deep-hearted, pure, with scented dew still wet—
   One perfect rose.

I knew the language of the floweret;
   "My fragile leaves," it said, "his heart enclose."
Love long has taken for his amulet
   One perfect rose.

Why is it no one ever sent me yet
   One perfect limousine, do you suppose?
Ah no, it's always just my luck to get
   One perfect rose.

— DOROTHY PARKER

A Mad Answer
of a Madman

One asked a madman if a wife he had.
"A wife?" quoth he. "I never was so mad."

— ROBERT HAYMAN

Spring

When daisies pied and violets blue,
  And lady-smocks all silver-white,
And cuckoo-buds of yellow hue
  Do paint the meadows with delight,
The cuckoo then, on every tree,
Mocks married men; for thus sings he,
                    "Cuckoo!
Cuckoo, cuckoo!" O word of fear,
Unpleasing to a married ear!

When shepherds pipe on oaten straws,
  And merry larks are ploughmen's clocks,
When turtles tread, and rooks, and daws,
  And maidens bleach their summer smocks,
The cuckoo then, on every tree,
Mocks married men; for thus sings he,
                    "Cuckoo!
Cuckoo, cuckoo!" O word of fear,
Unpleasing to a married ear!

— WILLIAM SHAKESPEARE

Dirty No-Gooder Blues

Did you ever fall in love with a man that was no
    good
Did you ever fall in love with a man that was no
    good
No matter what you did for him he never under-
    stood
The meanest things he could say would thrill you
    through and through

The meanest things he could say would thrill you
    through and through
And there was nothing too dirty for that man to
    do

He'd treat you nice and kind 'til he'd win your
    heart in hand
He'd treat you nice and kind 'til he'd win your
    heart in hand
Then he'd get so cruel that man you just could
    not stand

Lord, I really don't think no man love can last
Lord, I don't think no man love can last
They love you to death then treat you like a thing
  of the past

There's nineteen men living in my neighborhood
There's nineteen men living in my neighborhood
Eighteen of them are fools and the one ain't no
  doggone good

Lord, lord, lord, lord, lord, oh lord, lord lord
That dirty no-good man treats me just like I'm a
  dog

— BESSIE SMITH

Marriage Counsel

Marriage counselor said to me,
"You know your Edgar loves you.
It happens with a man sometimes.
Okay! A few lost days now and then
But he'll be back again.
His heart is home with you!
Trust me!"
I said,
"I know home is where his *heart* is
But damn that!
I wanna be where the rest of him is at."

— RUBY DEE

An Argument

I've oft been told by learned friars,
   That wishing and the crime are one,
And Heaven punishes desires
   As much as if the deed were done.

If wishing damns us, you and I
   Are damned to all our heart's content;
Come, then, at least we may enjoy
   Some pleasure for our punishment!

      — THOMAS MOORE

Get It & Feel Good

you cd just take what
he's got for you
i mean what's available
cd add up in the long run
if it's music/ take it
say he's got good
dishwashing techniques
he cd be a marvelous
masseur/ take it
whatever good there is to
get/ get it & feel good

say there's an electrical
wiring fanatic/ he cd
come in handy some day
suppose they know how to tend plants
if you want somebody
with guts/ you cd go to a rodeo
a prize fight/ or a gang war might be up your alley
there's somebody out there
with something you want/
not alla it/ but a lil
bit from here & there can
add up in the long run

whatever good there is to get
get it & feel good
this one's got kisses
that one can lay
linoleum
this one likes wine
that one fries butter fish
real good
this one is a anarcho-musicologist
this one wants pushkin to rise again
& that one has had it with the past tense/
whatever good there is to get/
get it & feel good
this one cd make music
roll around the small of
yr back & that one jumps
up & down in the gardens
it cd be yrs
there really is enuf to get
by with in this world but
you have to know what yr looking
for/ whatever good there is to get
get it & feel good
you have to know what

they will give up easily
what's available is not always
all that's possible
but there's so much fluctuation
in the market these days
you have to be
particular
whatever good there is to get
get it & feel good

whatever good there is to get
get it & feel good/ get it & feel good
snatch it & feel good
grab it & feel good
steal it & feel good
borrow it & feel good
reach it & feel good
you cd
    oh yeah
      & feel good.

— NTOZAKE SHANGE

Me and My
Chauffeur Blues

Won't you be my chauffeur
Won't you by my chauffeur
I want someone to drive me
I want someone to drive me
Down town
Baby drives so easy
I can't turn him down

But I don't want him
But I don't want him
To be riding these girls
To be riding these girls
A-round
You know I'm gonna steal me a pistol
Shoot my chauffeur down

Well I must buy him
Well I must buy him
A brand new V-8
A brand new V-8 Ford
And he won't need no passengers
I will be his load

(Yeah, take it away)

Going to let my chauffeur
Going to let my chauffeur
Drive me around the
Drive me around the
World
Then he can be my little boy
Yes I'll treat him good

— MEMPHIS MINNIE

Song

Pious Selinda goes to prayers,
   If I but ask the favour;
And yet the tender fool's in tears,
   When she believes I'll leave her.

Would I were free from this restraint,
   Or else had hopes to win her;
Would she could make of me a saint,
   Or I of her a sinner.

— WILLIAM CONGREVE

The Constant Lover

Out upon it! I have loved
    Three whole days together;
And am like to love three more,
    If it prove fair weather.

Time shall moult away his wings,
    Ere he shall discover
In the whole wide world again
    Such a constant lover.

But the spite on 't is, no praise
    Is due at all to me:
Love with me had made no stays
    Had it any been but she.

Had it any been but she,
    And that very face,
There had been at least ere this
    A dozen dozen in her place.

— SIR JOHN SUCKLING

A Man's Requirements

I

Love me Sweet, with all thou art,
  Feeling, thinking, seeing;
Love me in the lightest part,
  Love me in full being.

II

Love me with thine open youth
  In its frank surrender;
With the vowing of thy mouth,
  With its silence tender.

III

Love me with thine azure eyes,
  Made for earnest granting;
Taking colour from the skies,
  Can Heaven's truth be wanting?

IV

Love me with their lids, that fall
   Snow-like at first meeting;
Love me with thine heart, that all
   Neighbours then see beating.

V

Love me with thine hand stretched out
   Freely—open-minded:
Love me with thy loitering foot,—
   Hearing one behind it.

VI

Love me with thy voice, that turns
   Sudden faint above me;
Love me with thy blush that burns
   When I murmur *Love me!*

VII

Love me with thy thinking soul,
   Break it to love-sighing;
Love me with thy thoughts roll
   On through living—dying.

VIII

Love me when in thy gorgeous airs,
    When the world has crowned thee;
Love me, kneeling at thy prayers,
    With the angels round thee.

IX

Love me pure, as musers do,
    Up the woodlands shady:
Love me gaily, fast and true,
    As a winsome lady.

X

Through all hopes that keep us brave,
    Farther off or nigher,
Love me for the house and grave,
    And for something higher.

XI

Thus, if thou wilt prove me, Dear,
    Woman's love no fable,
I will love *thee*—half a year—
    As a man is able.

— ELIZABETH BARRETT BROWNING

The Ruined Maid

"O 'Melia, my dear, this does everything crown!
Who could have supposed I should meet you in
   Town?
And whence such fair garments, such
   prosperi-ty?"—
"O didn't you know I'd been ruined?" said she.

—"You left us in tatters, without shoes or socks,
Tired of digging potatoes, and spudding up docks;
And now you've gay bracelets and bright feathers
   three!"
"Yes: that's how we dress when we're ruined," said
she.

—"At home in the barton you said 'thee' and
'thou,' and 'thik oon,' and 'theäs oon,' and 't'other';
   but now
Your talking quite fits 'ee for high compa-ny!"—
"Some polish is gained with one's ruin," said she.

—"Your hands were like paws then, your face
   blue and bleak
But now I'm bewitched by your delicate cheek,

And your little gloves fit as on any la-dy!"—
"We never do work when we're ruined," said she.

—"You used to call home-life a hag-ridden dream,
And you'd sigh, and you'd sock; but at present
  you seem
To know not of megrims or melancho-ly!"
"True. One's pretty lively when ruined," said she.

—"I wish I had feathers, a fine sweeping gown,
And delicate face, and could strut about Town!"—
"My dear—a raw country girl, such as you be,
Cannot quite expect that. You ain't ruined," said
  she.

— THOMAS HARDY

Song

When lovely woman stoops to folly,
    And finds too late that men betray,
What charm can soothe her melancholy;
    What art can wash her guilt away?

The only art her guilt to cover,
    To hide her shame from every eye,
To give repentance to her lover,
    And wring his bosom—is to die.

— OLIVER GOLDSMITH

When I Was One-And-Twenty

When I was one-and-twenty
    I heard a wise man say,
"Give crowns and pounds and guineas
    But not your heart away;
Give pearls away and rubies
    But keep your fancy free."
But I was one-and-twenty,
    No use to talk to me.

When I was one-and-twenty
    I heard him say again,
"The heart out of the bosom
    Was never given in vain;
'Tis paid with sighs a plenty
    And sold for endless rue."
And I am two-and-twenty,
    And oh, 'tis true, 'tis true.

—A. E. HOUSMAN

As Love and I

As Love and I, late harbour'd in one inn,
With proverbs thus each other entertain:
In love there is no lack, thus I begin,
Fair words make fools, replieth he again;
Who spares to speak, doth spare to speed (quoth I),
As well (saith he) too forward, as too slow;
Fortune assists the boldest, I reply,
A hasty man (quoth he) ne'er wanted woe;
Labour is light, where love (quoth I) doth pay,
(Saith he) light burthen's heavy, if far born;
(Quoth I) the main lost, cast the bye away;
You have spun a fair thread, he replies in scorn.
    And having thus awhile each other thwarted,
    Fools as we met, so fools again we parted.

— MICHAEL DRAYTON

Friday Night

Love, the sole Goddess fit for swearing by,
Concedes us graciously the little lie:
The white lie, the half-lie, the lie corrective
Without which love's exchange might prove
  defective,
Confirming hazardous relationships
By kindly *maquillage* of Truth's pale lips.

This little lie was first told, so they say,
On the sixth day (Love's planetary day)
When, meeting her full-bosomed and half
  dressed,
Jove roared out suddenly: "Hell take the rest!
Six hard days of Creation are enough"—
And clasped her to him, meeting no rebuff.

Next day he rested, and she rested too.
The busy little lie between them flew:
"If this be not perfection," love would sigh,
"Perfection is a great, black, thumping lie…"
Endearments, kisses, grunts, and whispered
  oaths;
But were her thoughts on breakfast, or on
  clothes?

— ROBERT GRAVES

Loss

The day he moved was terrible—
That evening she went through hell.
His absence wasn't a problem
But the corkscrew had gone as well.

— WENDY COPE

Oh, When I Was
In Love With You

Oh, when I was in love with you,
  Then I was clean and brave,
And miles around the wonder grew
  How well did I behave.

And now the fancy passes by,
  And nothing will remain,
And miles around they'll say that I
  Am quite myself again.

— A. E. HOUSMAN

Fleeting Love

Give All to Love

Give all to love;
Obey thy heart;
Friends, kindred, days,
Estate, good fame,
Plans, credit, and the muse;
Nothing refuse.

'Tis a brave master,
Let it have scope,
Follow it utterly,
Hope beyond hope;
High and more high,
It dives into noon,
With wing unspent,
Untold intent;
But 'tis a god,
Knows its own path,
And the outlets of the sky.

'Tis not for the mean,
It requireth courage stout,
Souls above doubt,
Valor unbending;
Such 'twill reward,
They shall return
More than they were,
And ever ascending.

Leave all for love;—
Yet, hear me, yet,
One word more thy heart behoved,
One pulse more of firm endeavor,
Keep thee to-day,
To-morrow, for ever,
Free as an Arab
Of thy beloved.
Cling with life to the maid;
But when the surprise,
Vague shadow of surmise,

Flits across her bosom young
Of a joy apart from thee,
Free be she, fancy-free,
Do not thou detain a hem,

Nor the palest rose she flung
From her summer diadem.

Though thou loved her as thyself,
As a self of purer clay,
Tho' her parting dims the day,
Stealing grace from all alive,
Heartily know,
When half-gods go,
The gods arrive.

— RALPH WALDO EMERSON

To His Coy Mistress

Had we but world enough, and time,
This coyness, Lady, were no crime.
We would sit down and think which way
To walk and pass our long love's day.
Thou by the Indian Ganges' side
Shouldst rubies find: I by the tide
Of Humber would complain. I would
Love you ten years before the Flood,
And you should, if you please, refuse
Till the conversion of the Jews.
My vegetable love should grow
Vaster than empires, and more slow;
An hundred years should go to praise
Thine eyes and on thy forehead gaze;
Two hundred to adore each breast;
But thirty thousand to the rest;
An age at least to every part,
And the last age should show your heart;
For, Lady, you deserve this state,
Nor would I love at lower rate.
  But at my back I always hear
Time's wingèd chariot hurrying near;
And yonder all before us lie
Deserts of vast eternity.

Thy beauty shall no more be found,
Nor, in thy marble vault, shall sound
My echoing song: then worms shall try
That long preserved virginity,
And your quaint honour turn to dust,
And into ashes all my lust:
The grave's a fine and private place,
But none, I think, do there embrace.
  Now therefore, while the youthful hue
Sits on thy skin like morning dew,
And while thy willing soul transpires
At every pore with instant fires,
Now let us sport us while we may,
And now, like amorous birds of prey,
Rather at once our time devour
Than languish in his slow-chapt power.
Let us roll all our strength and all
Our sweetness up into one ball,
And tear our pleasures with rough strife
Thorough the iron gates of life:
Thus, though we cannot make our sun
Stand still, yet we will make him run.

— ANDREW MARVELL

Come, My Celia

Come, my Celia, let us prove
While we may, the sports of love;
Time will not be ours forever;
He at length our good will sever.
Spend not then his gifts in vain.
Suns that set may rise again;
But if once we lose this light,
'Tis with us perpetual night.
Why should we defer our joys?
Fame and rumor are but toys.
Cannot we delude the eyes
Of a few poor household spies,
Or his easier ears beguile,
So removed by our wile?
'Tis no sin love's fruit to steal;
But the sweet theft to reveal.
To be taken, to be seen,
These have crimes accounted been.

— BEN JONSON

"It was a lover and his lass"

It was a lover and his lass,
  With a hey, and a ho, and a hey nonino,
That o'er the green cornfield did pass,
  In the spring time, the only pretty ring time,
When birds do sing, hey ding a ding, ding;
Sweet lovers love the spring.

Between the acres of the rye,
  With a hey, and a ho, and a hey nonino,
These pretty country folks would lie,
  In the spring time, etc.

This carol they began that hour,
  With a hey, and a ho, and a hey nonino,
How that a life was but a flower
  In the spring time, etc.

And therefore take the present time,
  With a hey, and a ho, and a hey nonino;
For love is crowned with the prime
  In the spring time, etc.

— WILLIAM SHAKESPEARE

Love's Emblems

Now the lusty spring is seen;
  Golden yellow, gaudy blue,
  Daintily invite the view:
Everywhere on every green
Roses blushing as they blow
  And enticing men to pull,
Lilies whiter than the snow,
  Woodbines of sweet honey full:
    All love's emblems, and all cry,
    "Ladies, if not plucked, we die."

Yet the lusty spring hath stayed;
  Blushing red and purest white
  Daintily to love invite
Every woman, every maid:
Cherries kissing as they grow,
  And inviting men to taste,
Apples even ripe below,
  Winding gently to the waist:
    All love's emblems, and all cry,
    "Ladies, if not plucked, we die."

— JOHN FLETCHER

To the Virgins,
to Make Much of Time

Gather ye rosebuds while ye may,
Old Time is still a-flying:
And this same flower that smiles today
Tomorrow will be dying.

The glorious lamp of heaven, the sun,
The higher he's a-getting,
The sooner will his race be run,
And nearer he's to setting.

That age is best which is the first,
When youth and blood are warmer;
But being spent, the worse, and worst
Times still succeed the former.

Then be not coy, but use your time;
And while ye may, go marry;
For having lost but once your prime,
You may for ever tarry.

— ROBERT HERRICK

Feste's Song
(*from* *Twelfth Night*)

O mistress mine, where are you roaming?
O! stay and hear; your true love's coming,
   That can sing both high and low.
Trip no further, pretty sweeting;
Journeys end in lovers meeting,
   Every wise man's son doth know.

What is love? 'Tis not hereafter:
Present mirth hath present laughter;
   What's to come is still unsure.
In delay there lies no plenty;
Then come kiss me, sweet and twenty;
   Youth's a stuff will not endure.

— WILLIAM SHAKESPEARE

"Go, lovely rose"

Go, lovely Rose—
    Tell her that wastes her time and me,
    That now she knows,
When I resemble her to thee,
How sweet and fair she seems to be.

    Tell her that's young,
And shuns to have her graces spied,
    That hadst thou sprung
In deserts where no men abide,
Thou must have uncommended died.

    Small is the worth
Of beauty from the light retired:
    Bid her come forth,
Suffer herself to be desired,
And not blush so to be admired

    Then die—that she
The common fate of all things rare
    May read in thee;
How small a part of time they share
That are so wondrous sweet and fair!

— EDMUND WALLER

Love and Friendship

Love is like the wild rose-briar,
Friendship like the holly-tree—
The holly is dark when the rose-briar blooms
But which will bloom most constantly?

The wild rose-briar is sweet in spring,
Its summer blossoms scent the air;
Yet wait till winter comes again
And who will call the wild-briar fair?

Then scorn the silly rose-wreath now
And deck thee with the holly's sheen,
That when December blights thy brow
He still may leave thy garland green.

— EMILY BRONTË

Come, Fill the Cup

Come, fill the cup, and in the fire of spring
Your winter garment of repentance fling.
The bird of time has but a little way
To flutter—and the bird is on the wing.

— OMAR KHÁYYAM

Of Beauty

Let us use it while we may
Snatch those joys that haste away!
Earth her winter coat may cast,
And renew her beauty past:
But, our winter come, in vain
We solicit spring again;
And when our furrows snow shall cover,
Love may return but never lover.

— SIR RICHARD FANSHAWE

Love and Life

All my past life is mine no more;
  The flying hours are gone,
Like transitory dreams given o'er
Whose images are kept in store
  By memory alone.

Whatever is to come is not:
  How can it then be mine?
The present moment's all my lot,
And that, as fast as it got,
  Phyllis, is wholly thine.

Then talk not of inconstancy,
  False hearts, and broken vows;
If I, by miracle, can be
This livelong minute true to thee,
  'Tis all that heaven allows.

— JOHN WILMOT, EARL OF ROCHESTER

"False though she be
to me and love"

False though she be to me and love,
   I'll ne'er pursue revenge;
For still the charmer I approve,
   Though I deplore her change.

In hours of bliss we oft have met;
   They could not always last:
And though the present I regret,
I'm grateful for the past.

— WILLIAM CONGREVE

Jenny Kiss'd Me

Jenny kiss'd me when we met,
    Jumping from the chair she sat in;
Time, you thief, who love to get
    Sweets into you list, put that in!
Say I'm weary, say I'm sad,
    Say that health and wealth have miss'd me,
Say I'm growing old, but add,
    Jenny kiss'd me.

— LEIGH HUNT

The Look

Strephon kissed me in the spring,
   Robin in the fall,
But Colin only looked at me
   And never kissed at all.

Strephon's kiss was lost in jest,
   Robin's lost in play,
But the kiss in Colin's eyes
   Haunts me night and day.

— SARA TEASDALE

Corinne's Last Love Song

I

How beautiful, how beautiful you streamed
upon my sight,
In glory and in grandeur, as a gorgeous
sunset-light!
How softly, soul-subduing, fell your words
upon mine ear,
Like low aerial music when some angel
hovers near!
What tremulous, faint ecstasy to clasp your
hand in mine,
Till the darkness fell upon me of a glory too
divine!
The air around grew languid with our
intermingled breath,
And in your beauty's shadow I sank motion-
less as death.
I saw you not, I heard not, for a mist was
on my brain—
I only felt that life could give no joy like
that again.

II

And this was Love, I knew it not, but blindly floated on,

And now I'm on the ocean waste, dark, desolate, alone;

The waves are raging round me—I'm reckless where they guide;

No hope is left to right me, no strength to stem the tide.

As a leaf along the torrent, a cloud across the sky,

As dust upon the whirlwind, so my life is drifting by.

The dream that drank the meteor's light—the form from Heav'n has flown—

The vision and the glory, they are passing—they are gone.

Oh! love is frantic agony, and life one throb of pain;

Yet I would bear its darkest woes to dream that dream again.

— JANE FRANCESCA, LADY WILDE

The Indifferent

I can love both fair and brown,
Her whom abundance melts, and her whom want
  betrays,
Her who loves loneness best, and her who masks
  and plays,
  Her whom the country formed, and whom the
town,
    Her who believes, and her who tries,
    Her who still weeps with spongy eyes,
  And her who is dry cork, and never cries;
  I can love her, and her, and you and you,
  I can love any, so she be not true.

    Will no other vice content you?
Will it not serve your turn to do, as did your
  mothers?
Or have you old vices spent, and now would find
  out others?
    Or doth a fear, that men are true, torment you?

    Oh we are not, be not you so,
    Let me, and do you, twenty know.
  Rob me, but bind me not, and let me go.

Must I, who came to travail thorough you,
Grow your fixed subject, because you are true?

Venus heard me sigh this song,
And by Love's sweetest part, variety, she swore,
She heard not this till now; and and't should be
  so no more
    She went, examined, and returned ere long,
      And said, alas, Some two or three
      Poor heretics in love there be,
    Which think to 'stablish dangerous constancy.
    But I have told them, since you will be true,
    You shall be true to them, who are false to you.

— JOHN DONNE

"The dewdrop"

The dewdrop
on a bamboo leaf
stays longer
than you, who vanish
at dawn.

— IZUMI SHIKIBU

The String
Around My Finger

The bell that strikes the warning hour,
Reminds me that I should not linger,
And winds around my heart its power,
Tight as the string around my finger.

A sweet good-night I give, and then
Far from my thoughts I need must fling her,
Who blessed that lovely evening, when
She tied the string around my finger.

Lovely and virtuous, kind and fair,
A sweet-toned bell, O! who shall ring her!
Of her let bell men all beware,
Who ties such strings around their finger.

What shall I do?—I'll sit me down,
And, in my leisure hours, I'll sing her
Who gave me neither smile nor frown,
But tied a thread around my finger.

Now may the quiet star-lit hours
Their gentlest dews and perfumes bring her;
And morning show its sweetest flowers
To her whose string is round my finger.

And never more may I forget
The spot where I so long did linger;—
But watch another chance, and get
Another string around my finger.

— JOHN BRAINARD

Down by the Salley Gardens

Down by the salley gardens my love and I did
  meet;
She passed the salley gardens with little snow-
  white feet.
She bid me take love easy, as the leaves grow on
  the tree;
But I, being young and foolish, with her would
  not agree.
In a field by the river my love and I did stand,
And on my leaning shoulder she laid her snow-
  white hand.
She bid me take life easy, as the grass grows on
  the weirs;
But I was young and foolish, and now am full of
  tears.

— W. B. YEATS

A Dream
Within a Dream

Take this kiss upon the brow!
And, in parting from you now,
Thus much let me avow—
You are not wrong, who deem
That my days have been a dream:
Yet if hope has flown away
In a night, or in a day,
In a vision, or in none,
Is it therefore the less *gone?*
All that we see or seem
Is but a dream within a dream.

I stand amid the roar
Of a surf-tormented shore,
And I hold within my hand
Grains of the golden sand—
How few! yet how they creep
Through my fingers to the deep,
While I weep—while I weep!
O God! can I not grasp
Them with a tighter clasp?
O God! can I not save
One from the pitiless wave?
Is *all* that we see or seem
But a dream within a dream?

— EDGAR ALLAN POE

The Revelation

An idle poet, here and there,
Looks around him; but, for all the rest,
The world, unfathomably fair,
Is duller than a witling's jest.
Love wakes men, once a lifetime each;
They lift their heavy lids, and look;
And, lo, what one sweet page can teach,
They read with joy, then shut the book.
And some give thanks, and some blaspheme
And most forget; but, either way,
That and the Child's unheeded dream
Is all the light of all their day.

— COVENTRY PATMORE

213

"Fear no more
the heat o' the sun"

Fear no more the heat o' the sun,
  Nor the furious winter's rages;
Thou thy worldly task hast done,
  Home art gone, and ta'en thy wages.
Golden lads and girls all must,
As chimney-sweepers, come to dust.

Fear no more the frown o' the great;
  Thou art past the tyrant's stroke;
Care no more to clothe and eat;
To thee the reed is as the oak.
The scepter, learning, physic, must
All follow this, and come to dust.

Fear no more the lightning-flash,
  Nor the all-dreaded thunder-stone;
Fear not slander, censure rash;
  Thou hast finished joy and moan.
All lovers young, all lovers must
Consign to thee, and come to dust.

— WILLIAM SHAKESPEARE

To an Inconstant One

I loved thee once; I'll love no more—
  Thine be the grief as is the blame;
Thou art not what thou wast before,
  What reason I should be the same?
    He that can love unloved again,
    Hath better store of love than brain:
God send me love my debts to pay,
While unthrifts fool their love away!

Nothing could have my love o'erthrown
  If thou hadst still continued mine;
Yea, if thou hadst remain'd thy own,
  I might perchance have yet been thine.
    But thou thy freedom didst recall
    That it thou might elsewhere enthral:
And then how could I but disdain
A captive's captive to remain?

When new desires had conquer'd thee
    And changed the object of thy will,
It had been lethargy in me,
    Not constancy, to love thee still.
        Yea, it had been a sin to go
        And prostitute affection so:
    Since we are taught no prayers to say
    To such as must to others pray.

Yet do thou glory in thy choice—
    Thy choice of his good fortune boast;
I'll neither grieve nor yet rejoice
    To see him gain what I have lost:
        The height of my disdain shall be
        To laugh at him, to blush for thee;
    To love thee still, but go no more
    A-begging at a beggar's door.

— SIR ROBERT AYTON

*Enduring
Love*

My True-Love Hath My Heart, and I Have His

My true-love hath my heart, and I have his,
By just exchange one for another given:
I hold his dear, and mine he cannot miss,
There never was a better bargain driven:

My true-love hath my heart, and I have his,
My heart in me keeps him and me in one,
My heart in him his thoughts and senses guide:
He loves my heart, for once it was his own,
I cherish his because in me it bides:

My true-love hath my heart, and I have his.

— SIR PHILIP SIDNEY

"Love Me Not"

Love not me for comely grace,
For my pleasing eye or face;
Nor for any outward part,
No, nor for my constant heart:
  For those may fail or turn to ill,
  So thou and I shall sever.
Keep therefore a true woman's eye,
And love me still, but know not why;
  So hast thou the same reason still
  To doat upon me ever.

— JOHN WILBYE

"Believe me, if all those endearing young charms"

Believe me, if all those endearing young charms,
    Which I gaze on so fondly to-day,
Were to change by to-morrow, and fleet in my
  arms,
    Like fairy-gifts fading away,
Thou wouldst still be adored, as this moment
  thou art,
    Let thy loveliness fade as it will,
And around the dear ruin each wish of my heart
    Would entwine itself verdantly still.

It is not while beauty and youth are thine own,
    And thy cheeks unprofaned by a tear,
That the fervor and faith of a soul may be known,
    To which time will but make thee more dear!
No, the heart that has truly loved never forgets,
    But as truly loves on to the close,
As the sunflower turns to her god when he sets
    The same look which she turned when he 'rose!

— THOMAS MOORE

221

The Irish Peasant
to His Mistress

Through grief and through danger thy smile hath
cheer'd my way,
Till hope seem'd to bud from each thorn that
round me lay;
The darker our fortune, the brighter our pure love
burn'd,
Till shame into glory, till fear into zeal was turn'd:
Yes, slave as I was, in thy arms my spirit felt free,
And bless'd even the sorrows that made me more
dear to thee.

Thy rival was honour'd, while thou wert wrong'd
and scorn'd;
Thy crown was of briers, while gold her brows
adorn'd;
She woo'd me to temples, whilst thou lay'st hid in
caves;
Her friends were all masters, while thine, alas!
were slaves;

Yet cold in the earth, at thy feet, I would rather be
Than wed what I loved not, or turn one thought
  from thee.

They slander thee sorely, who say thy vows are
  frail—
Hadst thou been a false one, thy cheek had look'd
  less pale!
They say, too, so long thou hast worn those
  lingering chains,
That deep in thy heart they have printed their
  servile stains:
O, foul is the slander!—no chain could that soul
  subdue—
Where shineth thy spirit, there Liberty shineth
  too!

— THOMAS MOORE

Delia

When winter snows upon thy golden hairs,
And frost of age hath nipped thy flowers near;
When dark shall seem thy day that never clears,
And all lies with'red that was held so dear;
Then take this picture which I here present thee,
Limned with a pencil not all unworthy.
Here see the gifts that God and nature lent thee;
Here read thy self and what I suff'red for thee.
This may remain thy lasting monument,
Which happily posterity may cherish.
These colors with thy fading are not spent;
These may remain when thou and I shall perish.
If they remain, then thou shalt live thereby:
They will remain, and so thou canst not die.

— SAMUEL DANIEL

Beauty That Is Never Old

When buffeted and beaten by life's storms,
When by the bitter cares of life oppressed,
I want no surer haven than your arms,
I want no sweeter heaven than your breast.

When over my life's way there falls the blight
Of sunless days, and nights of starless skies;
Enough for me, the calm and steadfast light
That softly shines within your loving eyes.

The world, for me, and all the world can hold
Is circled by your arms; for me there lies,
Within the lights and shadows of your eyes,
The only beauty that is never old.

— JAMES WELDON JOHNSON

Love Is Enough: Song I

Love is enough: though the World be a-waning,
And the woods have no voice but the voice of
    complaining,
  Though the sky be too dark for dim eyes to
discover
The gold-cups and daisies fair blooming
  thereunder,
Though the hills be held shadows, and the sea a
    dark wonder,
  And this day draw a veil over all deeds pass'd
over,
Yet their hands shall not tremble, their feet shall
  · not falter:
The void shall not weary, the fear shall not alter
  These lips and these eyes of the loved and the
lover.

— WILLIAM MORRIS

I Corinthians 13

Though I speak with the tongues of men and of
angels, and have not charity, I am become as
the sounding brass, or a tinkling cymbal.

And though I have the gift of prophecy, and
understand all mysteries, and all knowledge;
and though I have all faith, so that I could
remove mountains, and have not charity, I am
nothing.

And though I bestow all my goods to feed the
poor, and though I give my body to be burned,
and have not charity, it profiteth me nothing.

Charity suffereth long, and is kind; charity envi-
eth not; charity vaunteth not itself, is not
puffed up,

Doth not behave itself unseemly, seeketh not her
own, is not easily provoked, thinketh no evil;

Rejoiceth not in iniquity but rejoiceth in the
truth;

Beareth all things, believeth all things, hopeth all things, endureth all things.

Charity never faileth; but whether there be prophecies, they shall fail; whether there be tongues, they shall cease; whether there be knowledge, it shall vanish away.

For we know in part, and we prophesy in part,

But when that which is perfect is come, that which is in part shall be done away.

When I was a child, I spake as a child, I understood as a child, I thought as a child; but when I became a man, I put away childish things.

For now we see through a glass, darkly; but then face to face; now I know in part; but then shall I know even as also I am known.

And now abideth faith, hope, charity, these three; but the greatest of these is charity.

— *from* THE AUTHORIZED VERSION

Love Lives

Love lives beyond
The tomb, the earth, which fades like dew.
I love the fond,
The faithful, and the true

Love lives in sleep,
The happiness of healthy dreams
Eve's dews may weep,
But love delightful seems.

'Tis heard in Spring
When light and sunbeams, warm and kind,
On angels' wing
Bring love and music to the mind.

And where is voice,
So young, so beautiful and sweet
As nature's choice,
Where Spring and lovers meet?

Love lives beyond
The tomb, the earth, the flowers, and dew.
I love the fond,
The faithful, young and true.

— JOHN CLARE

229

Only Our Love

Only our love hath no decay;
This, no tomorrow hath, nor yesterday,
Running it never runs from us away,
But truly keeps his first, last, everlasting day.

— JOHN DONNE

"One day I wrote her name upon the strand"

One day I wrote her name upon the strand,
  But came the waves and washèd it away:
Again I wrote it with a second hand,
  But came the tide, and made my pains his prey.
'Vain man,' said she, 'thou do'st in vain assay,
  A mortal thing so to immortalize,
For I myself shall like to this decay,
  And eek my name be wipèd out likewise.'
'Not so,' quoth I, 'let baser things devise
  To die in dust, but you shall live by fame:
My verse your virtues rare shall eternize,
  And in the heavens write your glorious name,
    Where, whenas death shall all the world subdue,
    Our love shall live, and later life renew.'

— EDMUND SPENSER

231

being to timelessness
as it's to time

being to timelessness as it's to time,
love did no more begin than love will end;
where nothing is to breathe to stroll to swim
love is the air the ocean and the land

(do lovers suffer?all divinities
proudly descending put on deathful flesh:
are lovers glad?only their smallest joy's
a universe emerging from a wish)

love is the voice under all silences,
the hope which has no opposite in fear;
the strength so strong mere force is feebleness:
the truth more first than sun more last than star

—do lovers love?why then to heaven with hell.
Whatever sages say and fools,all's well

— e. e. cummings

232

Most Sweet It Is

Most sweet it is with unuplifted eyes
To pace the ground, if path be there or none,
While a fair region 'round the traveller lies
Which he forbears again to look upon;
Pleased rather with some soft ideal scene,
The work of Fancy, or some happy tone
Of meditation, slipping in between
The beauty coming and the beauty gone.
If Thought and Love desert us, from that day
Let us break off all commerce with the Muse:
With Thought and Love companions of our way,
Whate'er the senses take or may refuse,
The Mind's internal heaven shall shed her dews
Of inspiration on the humblest lay.

— WILLIAM WORDSWORTH

Barter

Life has loveliness to sell,
  All beautiful and splendid things,
Blue waves whitened on a cliff,
  Soaring fire that sways and sings,
And children's faces looking up,
Holding wonder like a cup.

Life has loveliness to sell,
  Music like a curve of gold,
Scent of pine trees in the rain,
  Eyes that love you, arms that hold,
And for your spirit's still delight,
Holy thoughts that star the night.

Spend all you have for loveliness,
  Buy it and never count the cost;
For one white singing hour of peace
  Count many a year of strife well lost,
And for a breath of ecstasy
Give all you have been, or could be.

— SARA TEASDALE

In a Rose Garden

A hundred years from now, dear heart,
  We shall not care at all,
It will not matter then a whit,
  The honey or the gall.
The summer days that we have known
Will all forgotten be and flown;
The garden will be overgrown
  Where now the roses fall.

A hundred years from now, dear heart,
  We shall not mind the pain;
The throbbing crimson tide of life
  Will not have left a stain.
The song we sing together, dear,
The dream we dream together here,
Will mean no more than means a tear
  Amid a summer rain.

A hundred years from now, dear heart,
  The grief will all be o'er;
The sea of care will surge in vain
  Upon a careless shore.
These glasses we turn down today
Here at the parting of the way—
We shall be wineless then as they,
  And shall not mind it more.

A hundred years from now, dear heart,
  We'll neither know nor care
What came of all life's bitterness,
  Or followed love's despair.
Then fill the glasses up again,
And kiss me through the rose-leaf rain;
We'll build one castle more in Spain,
  And dream one more dream there.

— JOHN BENNETT

Love Thyself Last

Love thyself last. Look near, behold thy duty
To those who walk beside thee down life's road;
Make glad their days by little acts of beauty,
And them bear the burden of earth's load.

Love thyself last. Look far and find the stranger,
Who staggers 'neath his sin and his despair;
Go lend a hand, and lead him out of danger,
To heights where he may see the world is fair.

Love thyself last. The vastnesses above thee
Are filled with Spririt Forces, strong and pure.
And fevently, these faithful friends shall love thee:
Keep thou thy watch o'er others, and endure.

Love thyself last; and oh, such joy shall thrill thee,
As never yet to selfish souls was given.
Whate'er thy lot, a perfect peace will fill thee,
And earth shall seem the ante-room of Heaven.

Love thyself last, and thou shall grow in spirit
To see, to hear, to know, and understand.
The message of the stars, lo, thou shall hear it,
And all God's joys shall be at thy command.

— ELLA WHEELER WILCOX

We Have Lived
and Loved Together

We have lived and loved together
   Through many changing years;
We have shared each other's gladness
   And wept each other's tears;
I have known ne'er a sorrow
   That was long unsoothed by thee;
For thy smiles can make a summer
   Where darkness else would be.

Like the leaves that fall around us
   In autumn's fading hours,
Are the traitor's smiles, that darken
   When the cloud of sorrow lowers;
And though many such we've known, love,
   Too prone, alas, to range,
We both can speak of one love
   Which time can never change.

We have lived and loved together
  Through many changing years,
We have shared each other's gladness
  And wept each other's tears.
And let us hope the future,
  As the past has been will be:
I will share with thee my sorrows,
  And thou thy joys with me.

— CHARLES JEFFERYS

Music

Music, when soft voices die,
Vibrates in the memory—
Odours, when sweet violets sicken,
Live within the sense they quicken.
Rose leaves, when the rose is dead,
Are heaped for the belovèd's bed;
And so thy thoughts, when thou art gone,
Love itself shall slumber on.

— PERCY BYSSHE SHELLEY

Absent
and Lost Love

Absent Yet Present

As the flight of a river
   That flows to the sea
My soul rushes ever
   In tumult to thee.

A twofold existence
   I am where thou art:
My heart in the distance
   Beats close to thy heart.

Look up, I am near thee,
   I gaze on thy face:
I see thee, I hear thee,
   I feel thine embrace.

As the magnet's control on
   The steel it draws to it,
Is the charm of thy soul on
   The thoughts that pursue it.

And absence but brightens
   The eyes that I miss,
And custom but heightens
   The spell of thy kiss.

It is not from duty,
    Though that may be owed,—
It is not from beauty,
    Though that be bestowed:

But all that I care for,
    And all that I know,
Is that, without wherefore,
    I worship thee so.

Through granite it breaketh
    A tree to the ray:
As a dreamer forsaketh
    The grief of the day,

My soul in its fever
    Escapes unto thee:
O dream to the griever!
    O light to the tree!

A twofold existence
    I am where thou art:
Hark, hear in the distance
    The beat of my heart!

— EDWARD BULWER-LYTTON

To F—

Beloved! amid the earnest woes
   That crowd around my earthly path—
(Drear path, alas! Where grows
not even one lonely rose)—
   My soul at least a solace hath
In dreams of thee, and therein knows
An Eden of bland repose.

And thus thy memory is to me
   Like some enchanted far-off isle
In some tumultuous sea—
Some ocean throbbing far and free
   With storms—but where meanwhile
Serenest skies continually
   Just o'er that one bright island smile.

— EDGAR ALLAN POE

After Parting

Oh I have sown my love so wide
That he will find it everywhere;
It will awake him in the night,
It will enfold him in the air.

I set my shadow in his sight
And I have winged it with desire,
That it may be a cloud by day
And in the night a shaft of fire.

— SARA TEASDALE

To Mary

I SLEEP with thee, and wake with thee,
And yet thou art not there;
I fill my arms with thoughts of thee,
And press the common air.
Thy eyes are gazing upon mine
When thou art out of sight;
My lips are always touching thine
At morning, noon, and night.

I think and speak of other things
To keep my mind at rest,
But still to thee my memory clings
Like love in woman's breast.
I hide it from the world's wide eye
And think and speak contrary,
But soft the wind comes from the sky
And whispers tales of Mary.

The night-wind whispers in my ear,
The moon shines on my face;
The burden still of chilling fear
I find in every place.
The breeze is whispering in the bush,
And the leaves fall from the tree,
All sighing on, and will not hush,
Some pleasant tales of thee.

— JOHN CLARE

Westron Wynde

Westron wynde when wyll thow blow
the smalle rayne downe can rayne
Chryst yf my love wer in my armys
and I yn my bed agayne

— ANONYMOUS

Love Is Love

The lowest trees have tops, the ant her gall,
 The fly her spleen, the little sparks their heat;
The slender hairs cast shadows, though but small,
 And bees have stings, although they be not
 great;
Seas have their source, and so have shallow
 springs;
And love is love, in beggars as in kings.

Where rivers smoothest run, deep are the fords;
 The dial stirs, yet none perceives it move;
The firmest faith is in the fewest words;
 The turtles cannot sing, and yet they love:
True hearts have eyes and ears, no tongues to
 speak;
They hear and see, and sigh, and then they break.

— Sir Edward Dyer

249

Light

The night has a thousand eyes,
  The day but one;
Yet the light of the bright world dies
  With the dying sun.

The mind has a thousand eyes,
  And the heart but one;
Yet the light of a whole life dies
  When its love is done.

— FRANCIS W. BOURDILLON

The Lost Mistress

All's over, then: does truth sound bitter
    As one at first believes?
Hark, 'tis the sparrows' good-night twitter
    About your cottage eaves!

And the leaf-buds on the vine are woolly,
    I noticed that, today;
One day more bursts them open fully
    —You know the red turns grey.

Tomorrow we meet the same then, dearest?
    May I take your hand in mine?
Mere friends are we,—well, friends the merest
    Keep much that I resign:

For each glance of the eye so bright and black,
    Though I keep with heart's endeavour,—
Your voice, when you wish the snowdrops back,
    Though it stay in my soul for ever!—

Yet I will but say what mere friends say,
    Or only a thought stronger;
I will hold your hand but as long as all may,
    Or so very little longer!

— ROBERT BROWNING

"Farewell! Thou art too dear for my possessing"

Farewell! thou art too dear for my possessing,
And like enough thou knowst thy estimate,
The charter of thy worth gives thee releasing:
My bonds in thee are all determinate.
For how do I hold thee but by thy granting,
And for that riches where is my deserving?
The cause of this fair gift in me is wanting,
And so my patent back again is swerving.
Thy self thou gav'st, thy own worth then not
    knowing,
Or me to whom thou gav'st it, else mistaking,
So thy great gift upon misprision growing,
Comes home again, on better judgement making.
    Thus have I had thee as a dream doth flatter,
    In sleep a King, but waking no such matter.

— WILLIAM SHAKESPEARE

"Since there's no help"

Since there's no help, come let us kiss and part—
Nay, I have done, you get no more of me;
And I am glad, yea, glad with all my heart,
That thus so cleanly I myself can free.
Shake hands for ever, cancel all our vows,
And when we meet at any time again,
Be it not seen in either of our brows
That we one jot of fomer love retain.
Now at the last gasp of Love's latest breath,
When, his pulse failing, Passion speechless lies,
When Faith is kneeling by his bed of death,
And Innocence is closing up his eyes—
      Now if thou would'st, when all have given
   him over,
      From death to life thou might'st him yet
   recover.

— MICHAEL DRAYTON

I Loved You

I loved you; even now I may confess,
   Some embers of my love their fire retain;
But do not let it cause you more distress,
   I do not want to sadden you again.
Hopeless and tonguetied, yet I loved you dearly
   With pangs the jealous and timid know;
So tenderly I loved you, so sincerely,
   I pray God grant another love you so.

—ALEXANDER PUSHKIN
translated by R. M. HEWITT

A Farewell

With all my will, but much against my heart,
We two now part.
My Very Dear,
Our solace is, the sad road lies so clear.
It needs no art,
With faint, averted feet
And many a tear,
In our opposed paths to persevere.
Go thou to East, I West.
We will not say
There's any hope, it is so far away.
But, O, my Best,
When the one darling of our widowhead,
The nursling Grief,
Is dead,
And no dews blur our eyes
To see the peach-bloom come in evening skies,
Perchance we may,
Where now this night is day,
And even through faith of still averted feet,
Making full circle of our banishment,
Amazed meet;
The bitter journey to the bourne so sweet
Seasoning the termless feast of our content
With tears of recognition never dry.

— COVENTRY PATMORE

On Monsieur's Departure

I grieve and do not show my discontent,
I love and yet am forced to seem to hate,
I do, yet dare not say I ever meant,
I seem stark mute but inwardly do prate.
  I am and not, I freeze and yet am burned,
  Since from myself another self I turned.

My care is like my shadow in the sun,
Follows me flying, flies when I pusue it,
Stands and lies by me, doth what I have done.
His too familiar care doth make me rue it.
  No means I find to rid him from my breast,
  Till by the end of things it be supprest.

Some gentler passion slide into my mind,
For I am soft and made of melting snow;
Or be more cruel, love, and so be kind.
Let me or float or sink, be high or low.
  Or let me live with some more sweet content.
  Or die and so forget what love ere meant.

— ELIZABETH I

256

A Valediction

If we must part,
   Then let it be like this;
Not heart on heart,
   Nor with the useless anguish of a kiss;
But touch mine hand and say:
"Until tomorrow or some other day,
   If we must part."

Words are so weak
   When love hath been so strong:
Let silence speak:
   "Life is a little while, and love is long;
A time to sow and reap,
And after harvest a long time to sleep,
   But words are weak."

— ERNEST DOWSON

The Banks O'Doon

Ye flowery banks o' bonie Doon,
    How can ye blume sae fair;
How can ye chant, ye little birds,
    And I sae fu' o' care!

Thou'll break my heart, thou bonie bird
    That sings upon the bough;
Thou minds me o' the happy days
    When my fause luve was true.

Thou'll break my heart, thou bonie bird
    That sings beside thy mate;
For sae I sat, and sae I sang,
    And wist na o' my fate.

Aft hae I rov'd by bonie Doon,
　　To see the wood-bine twine,
And ilka bird sang o' its love,
　　And sae did I o' mine.

Wi' lightsome heart I pu'd a rose
　　Frae aff its thorny tree,
And my fause luver staw the rose,
　　But left the thorn wi' me.

Wi' lightsome heart I pu'd a rose,
　　Upon a morn in June:
And sae I flourish'd on the morn,
　　And sae was pu'd or noon!

— ROBERT BURNS

Farewell, Love

Farewell, love, and all thy laws for ever,
Thy baited hooks shall tangle me no more;
Senec and Plato call me from thy lore
To perfect wealth, my wit for to endeavor,
In blind error when I did perserver,
Thy sharp repulse that pricketh aye so sore
Hath taught me to set in trifles no store,
And scape forth, since liberty is lever.
Therefore, farewell! Go trouble younger hearts,
And in me claim no more authority;
With idle youth go use thy property,
And thereon spend thy many brittle darts.
For hitherto though I have lost my time,
Me lusteth no longer rotten boughs to climb.

— Sir Thomas Wyatt

"He that hath no mistress"

He that hath no mistress must not wear a
favour.

He that woos a mistress must serve before he
have her.

He that hath no bed-fellow must lie alone,

And he that hath no lady must be content with
Joan.

And so must I, for why? Alas, my love and I are
parted.

False Cupid, I will have thee whipped, and have
thy mother carted.

— ANONYMOUS

261

Bhartṛhari

She who is always in my thoughts prefers
Another man, and does not think of me.
Yet he seeks for another's love, not hers;
And some poor girl is grieving for my sake.
   Why then, the devil take
Both her and him; and love; and her; and me.

— *Translated from* THE SANSKRIT BY JOHN BROUGH

When We Two Parted

When we two parted
    In silence and tears,
Half broken-hearted
    To sever for years,
Pale grew thy cheek and cold,
    Colder than thy kiss;
Truly that hour foretold
    Sorrow to this.

The dew of the morning
    Sunk chill on my brow—
It felt like the warning
    Of what I feel now.
Thy vows are all broken,
    And light is thy fame;
I hear thy name spoken,
    And share in its shame.

They name thee before me,
   A knell to mine ear;
A shudder comes o'er me—
   Why wert thou so dear?
They know not I knew thee,
   Who knew thee too well—
Long, long shall I rue thee,
   Too deeply to tell.

In secret we met—
   In silence I grieve,
That thy heart could forget,
   Thy spirit deceive.
If I should meet thee
   After long years,
How should I greet thee?—
   With silence and tears.

— GEORGE GORDON,
LORD BYRON

"My True Love Hath My Heart and I Have His"

None ever was in love with me but grief.
  She wooed me from the day that I was born;
She stole my playthings first, the jealous thief,
  And left me there forlorn.

The birds that in my garden would have sung,
  She scared away with her unending moan;
She slew my lovers too when I was young,
  And left me there alone.

Grief, I have cursed thee often—now at last
  To hate thy name I am no longer free;
Caught in thy bony arms and prisoned fast,
  I love no love but thee.

— MARY COLERIDGE

265

Kashmiri Song

Pale hands I love beside the Shalimar,
   Where are you now? Who lies beneath your
spell?
Whom do you lead on Rapture's Roadway, far,
   Before you agonize them in farewell?

Oh, pale dispenser of my Joys and Pains,
   Holding the doors of Heaven and of Hell,
How the hot blood rushed wildly through the
veins
   Beneath your touch, until you waved farewell.

Pale hands, pink-tipped, like Lotus buds that float
   On those cool waters where we used to dwell,
I would have rather felt you round my throat
   Crushing out life than waving me farewell!

— LAURENCE HOPE

Song (Love Arm'd)

Love in fantastic triumph sat
  Whilst bleedings hearts around him flow'd,
For whom fresh paines he did create,
  And strange tyrannic power he show'd;

From thy bright eyes he took his fire,
  Which round about in sport he hurl'd;
But 'twas from mine he took desire,
  Enough to undo the amorous world.

From me he took his sighs and tears,
  From thee his pride and cruelty;
From me his languishments and fears,
  And every killing dart from thee.

Thus thou and I the god have arm'd,
  And set him up a deity;
But my poor heart alone is harm'd,
  Whilst thine the victor is, and free.

— APHRA BEHN

O Do Not Love
Too Long

Sweetheart, do not love too long:
I loved long and long
And grew to be out of fashion
Like an old song.

All through the years of our youth
Neither could have known
Their own thought from the other's,
We were so much at one.

But O, in a minute she changed—
O do not love too long,
Or you will grow out of fashion
Like an old song.

— W. B. YEATS

"Farewell ungrateful traitor"

Farewell ungrateful traitor,
   Farewell my perjured swain,
Let never injured creature
   Believe a man again.
The pleasure of possessing
Surpasses all expressing,
But 'tis too short a blessing,
   And love too long a pain.

'Tis easy to deceive us
   In pity of your pain,
But when we love you leave us
   To rail at you in vain.
Before we have described it,
There is no bliss beside it,

But she that once has tried it
   Will never love again.

The passion you pretended
   Was only to obtain,
But when the charm is ended
   The charmer you disdain.
Your love by ours we measure
Till we have lost our treasure,
But dying is a pleasure,
   When living is a pain.

— JOHN DRYDEN

Bonny Barbara Allan

It was in and about the Martinmas time,
    When the green leaves were a-falling,
That Sir John Graeme in the west country
    Fell in love with Barbara Allan.

He sent his man down through the town,
    To the place where she was dwelling,
O haste, and come to my master dear,
    Gin ye be Barbara Allan.

O hooly, hooly rose she up,
    To the place where he was lying,
And when she drew the curtain by,
    Young man, I think you're dying.

O it's I'm sick, and very very sick,
   And 'tis a' for Barbara Allan.
O the better for me ye's never be,
   Tho' your heart's blood were a-spilling.

O dinna ye mind, young man, said she,
   When ye was in the tavern a-drinking,
That ye made the healths gae round and
   round,
   And slighted Barbara Allan?

He turn'd his face unto the wall,
   And death was with him dealing;
Adieu, adieu, my dear friends all,
   And be kind to Barbara Allan.

— Anonymous

To Mrs. M. A.
Upon Absence

'Tis now since I began to die
Four months, yet still I gasping live;
Wrapp'd up in sorrow do I lie,
   Hoping, yet doubting a reprieve.
Adam from Paradise expell'd
Just such a wretched being held.

'Tis not thy love I fear to lose,
   That will in spite of absence hold;
But 'tis the benefit and use
   Is lost, as in imprison'd gold:
Which though the sum be ne'er so great,
Enriches nothing but conceit.

What angry star then governs me
 That I must feel a double smart,
Prisoner to fate as well as thee;
 Kept from thy face, link'd to thy heart?
Because my love all love excels,
Must my grief have no parallels?

Sapless and dead as Winter here
 I now remain, and all I see
Copies of my wild state appear,
 But I am their epitome.
Love me no more, for I am grown
Too dead and dull for thee to own.

   — KATHERINE PHILIPS

My Life Closed Twice Before Its Close

My life closed twice before its close—
It yet remains to see
If Immortality unveil
A third event to me

So huge, so hopeless to conceive
As these that twice befell.
Parting is all we know of heaven,
And all we need of hell.

— EMILY DICKINSON

The Going

Why did you give no hint that night
That quickly after the morrow's dawn,
And calmly, as if indifferent quite,
You would close your term here, up and
  be gone
      Where I could not follow
      With wing of swallow
To gain one glimpse of you ever anon!

      Never to bid good-bye,
      Or lip me the softest call,
Or utter a wish for a word, while I
Saw morning harden upon the wall,
      Unmoved, unknowing
      That your great going
Had place that moment, and altered all.

Why do you make me leave the house
And think for a breath it is you I see
At the end of the alley of bending boughs
Where so often at dusk you used to be;
      Till in darkening dankness
      The yawning blankness
Of the perspective sickens me!

You were she who abode
    By those red-veined rocks far West.
You were the swan-necked one who rode
Along the beetling Beeny Crest,
    And, reining nigh me,
    Would muse and eye me,
While Life unrolled us its very best.

Why, then, latterly did we not speak,
Did we not think of those days long dead,
And ere your vanishing strive to seek
That time's renewal? We might have said,
    "In this bright spring weather
    We'll visit together
Those places that once we visited."

    Well, well! All's past amend,
    Unchangeable. It must go.
I seem but a dead man held on end
To sink down soon . . . O you could not know
    That such swift fleeing
    No soul foreseeing—
Not even I—would undo me so!

— THOMAS HARDY

Song

Sweetest love, I do not go
   For weariness of thee,
Nor in hope the world can show
   A fitter love for me;
     But since that I
Must die at last, 'tis best
To use myself in jest
   Thus by fained deaths to die.

Yesternight the sun went hence,
   And yet is here today,
He hath no desire nor sense,
   Nor half so short a way:
     Then fear not me,
But believe that I shall make
Speedier journeys, since I take
   More wings and spurs than he.

O how feeble is man's power,
   That if good fortune fall,
Cannot add another hour,
   Nor a lost hour recall!
     But come bad chance,
And we join to it our strength,

And we teach it art and length,
    Itself o'er us to advance.

When thou sigh'st, thou sigh'st not wind,
    But sigh'st my soul away,
When thou weep'st, unkindly kind,
    My life's blood doth decay.
      It cannot be
That thou lov'st me, as thou say'st,
If in thine my life thou waste,
    Thou art the best of me.

Let not thy divining heart
    Forethink me any ill,
Destiny may take thy part,
    And may thy fears fulfil;
      But think that we
Are but turned aside to sleep;
They who one another keep
    Alive, ne'er parted be.

— JOHN DONNE

Annabel Lee

It was many and many a year ago,
  In a kingdom by the sea,
That a maiden there lived whom you may know
  By the name of Annabel Lee;
And this maiden she lived with no other thought
  Than to love and be loved by me.

She was a child and *I* was a child
  In this kingdom by the sea,
But we loved with a love that was more than
  love—
  I and my Annabel Lee,
With a love that the wingèd seraphs of heaven
  Coveted her and me.

And this was the reason that, long ago,
  In this kingdom by the sea,
A wind blew out of a cloud by night
  Chilling my Annabel Lee;
So that her highborn kinsmen came
  And bore her away from me,
To shut her up in a sepulchre
  In this kingdom by the sea.

The angels, not half so happy in heaven,
　　Went envying her and me:
Yes! that was the reason (as all men know,
　　In this kingdom by the sea)
That the wind came out of the cloud, chilling
　　And killing my Annabel Lee.

But our love it was stronger by far than the love
　　Of those who were older than we—
　　Of many far wiser than we—
And neither the angels in heaven above,
　　Nor the demons down under the sea,
Can ever dissever my soul from the soul
　　Of the beautiful Annabel Lee:

For the moon never beams without bringing me
　dreams
　　Of the beautiful Annabel Lee;
And the stars never rise but I see the bright eyes
　　Of the beautiful Annabel Lee;
And so, all the night-tide, I lie down by the side
Of my darling, my darling, my life and my
　bride,
　　In the sepulchre there by the sea—
　　In her tomb by the side of the sea.

— EDGAR ALLAN POE

281

"No longer mourn for me when I am dead"

No longer mourn for me when I am dead
Than you shall hear the surly sullen bell
Give warning to the world that I am fled
From this vile world, with vilest worms to dwell.
Nay, if you read this line, remember not
The hand that writ it, for I love you so,
That I in your sweet thoughts would be forgot,
If thinking on me then should make you woe.
O, if, I say, you look upon this verse
When I perhaps compounded am with clay,
Do not so much as my poor name rehearse,
But let you love even with my life decay,
    Lest the wise world should look into your moan
    And mock you with me after I am gone.

— WILLIAM SHAKESPEARE

Unfulfilled Love

Song: I Hid My Love

I hid my love when young till I
Couldn't bear the buzzing of a fly;
I hid my love to my despite
Till I could not bear to look at light:
I dare not gaze upon her face
But left her memory in each place;
Where'er I saw a wild flower lie
I kissed and bade my love good-bye.

I met her in the greenest dells,
Where dewdrops pearl the wood bluebells;
The lost breeze kissed her bright blue eye,
The bee kissed and went singing by,
A sunbeam found a passage there,
A gold chain round her neck so fair;
As secret as the wild bee's song
She lay there all the summer long.

I hid my love in field and town
Till e'en the breeze would knock me down;
The bees seemed singing ballads o'er,
The fly's bass turned a lion's roar;
And even silence found a tongue,
To haunt me all the summer long;
The riddle nature could not prove
Was nothing else but secret love.

— JOHN CLARE

Midsummer

You loved me for a little,
　　Who could not love me long;
You gave me wings of gladness
　　And lent my spirit song.

You loved me for an hour
　　But only with your eyes;
Your lips I could not capture
　　By storm or by surprise.

Your mouth that I remember
　　With rush of sudden pain
As one remembers starlight
　　Or roses after rain . . .

Out of a world of laughter
　　Suddenly I am sad . . .
Day and night it haunts me,
　　The kiss I never had.

— SYDNEY KING RUSSELL

from *Thomas Ford's Music of Sundry Kinds*

There is a lady sweet and kind,
Was never face so pleas'd my mind;
I did but see her passing by,
And yet I love her till I die.

Her gesture, motion, and her smiles,
Her wit, her voice, my heart beguiles,
Beguiles my heart, I know not why,
And yet I love her till I die.

Her free behaviour, winning looks,
Will make a lawyer burn his books;
I touch'd her not, alas! not I,
And yet I love her till I die.

Had I her fast betwixt mine arms,
Judge you that think such sports were harms,
Were't any harm? no, no, fie, fie,
For I will love her till I die.

Should I remain confined there
So long as Phoebus in his sphere,
I to request, she to deny,
Yet would I love her till I die.

Cupid is winged and doth range,
Her country so my love doth change:
But change she earth, or change she sky,
Yet will I love her till I die.

— THOMAS FORD

The Lover

My eyes want to kiss your face.
I have no power over my eyes.
They just want to kiss your face.
I flow towards you out of my eyes,
a fine heat trembles round your shoulders,
it slowly dissolves your contours
and I am there with you, your mouth
and everywhere around you—
I have no power over my eyes.

I sit with my hands in my lap,
I shan't touch you and I'll never speak.
But my eyes kiss your face,
I rise out of myself and no-one can stop me,
I flow out and I'm invisible,
I cannot stop this unfathomable flowing,
this dazzle that knows neither end nor beginning—
but when at last you turn your eyes towards me,
your unaware, questioning, stranger's eyes,
I sink myself back into my hands
And take up my place again under my eyelids.

SOLVEIG VON SCHOULTZ,
translated by ANNE BORN

I Just Couldn't

I wanted to tell the whole world
About my love for you
But I just couldn't.
I wanted to dance my love
Sing it or write a poem
But I just couldn't.
I dreamed a fantastic dream
Of me in your arms
And a long warm kiss.
I wanted the cat to answer me back
When I held her and called your name.
But she just couldn't.
I tried to tell my little sister
About my love for you
So that her big eyes could look at me
The way I want you to
But she was asleep and so
I just couldn't.

My folks say I'm too young
To be falling in love.
I tried to change my heart
To make my mind stop thinking
About you so much.
But I just couldn't.
I wrote your name on all the pages
Of my diary.
I took a letter I wrote you
To the mailbox—
But I just couldn't.

— Hasna Muhammmad

If You But Knew

If you but knew
How all my days seem filled with dreams of you,
How sometimes in the silent night
Your eyes thrill through me with their tender
  light,
How oft I hear your voice when others speak,
How you 'mid other forms I seek—
Oh, love more real than though such dreams
  were true
If you but knew.

Could you but guess
How you alone make all my happiness,
How I am more than willing for your sake
To stand alone, give all and nothing take,
Nor chafe to think you bound while I am free,
Quite free, till death, to love you silently,
Could you but guess.

Could you but learn
How when you doubt my truth I sadly yearn
To tell you all, to stand for one brief space
Unfettered, soul to soul, as face to face,
To crown you king, my king, till life shall end,
My lover and likewise my truest friend,
Would you love me, dearest, as fondly in return,
Could you but learn?

— ANONYMOUS

Song

I saw thee on thy bridal day—
  When a burning blush came o'er thee,
Though happiness around thee lay,
  The world all love before thee:

And in thine eye a kindling light
  (Whatever it might be)
Was all on Earth my aching sight
  Of Loveliness could see.

That blush, perhaps, was maiden shame—
  As such it well may pass—
Though its glow hath raised a fiercer flame
  In the breast of him, alas!

Who saw thee on that bridal day,
  When that deep blush *would* come o'er thee,
Though happiness around thee lay,
  The world all love before thee.

— EDGAR ALLAN POE

I Do Not Love Thee

I do not love thee!—no! I do not love thee!
And yet when thou art absent I am sad;
    And envy even the bright blue sky above thee,
Whose quiet stars may see thee and be glad.

I do not love thee!—yet, I know not why,
Whate'er thou dost seems still well done, to me:
    And often in my solitude I sigh
That those I do love are not more like thee!

I do not love thee!—yet, when thou art gone,
I hate the sound (though those who speak be dear)
    Which breaks the lingering echo of the tone
Thy voice of music leaves upon my ear.

I do not love thee!—yet thy speaking eyes,
With their deep, bright, and most expressive blue,
    Between me and the midnight heaven arise,
Oftener than any eyes I ever knew.

I know I do not love thee! yet, alas!
Others will scarcely trust my candid heart;
    And oft I catch them smiling as they pass,
Because they see me gazing where thou art.

— CAROLINE ELIZABETH SARAH NORTON

To Celia

Drink to me only with thine eyes,
   And I will pledge with mine;
Or leave a kiss but in the cup
   And I'll not look for wine.
The thirst that from the soul doth rise
   Doth ask a drink divine;
But might I of Jove's nectar sup,
   I would not change for thine.

I sent thee late a rosy wreath,
   Not so much honouring thee
As giving it a hope that there
   It could not withered be;
But thou thereon didst only breathe,
   And sent'st it back to me;
Since when it grows, and smells, I swear,
   Not of itself but thee!

— BEN JONSON

Sonnet VI

Where the red wine-cup floweth, there art thou!
Where luxury curtains out the evening sky;—
Triumphant Mirth sits flush'd upon thy brow,
And ready laughter lurks within thine eye,
Where the long day declineth, lone I sit,
In idle thought, my listless hands entwined,
And, faintly smiling at remember'd wit,
Act the scene over to my musing mind.
In my lone dreams I hear thy eloquent voice,
I see the pleased attention of the throng,
And bid my spirit in thy joy rejoice,
Lest in love's selfishness I do thee wrong.
Ah! Midst that proud and mirthful company
Send'st *thou* no wondering thought to love and me?

— CAROLINE ELIZABETH SARAH NORTON

"I abide and abide and better abide"

I abide and abide and better abide
(And after the old proverb) the happy day;
And ever my lady to me doth say
"Let me alone and I will provide."
I abide and abide and tarry the tide,
And with abiding speed well ye may!
Thus do I abide I wot always
Not her obtaining nor yet denied.
Aye me! This long abiding
Seemeth to me as who sayeth
A prolonging of a dying death
Or refusing of a desired thing.
Much were it better for to be plain
Than to say "abide" and yet not obtain.

— Sir Thomas Wyatt

Valentines

(written for Miss L——'s
Valentine Parties)

To——.
We never met; yet to my soul
Thy name hath been a voice of singing,
And ever to thy glorious lays
The echoes of my heart are ringing.

We never met; yet is thy face,
Thy pictured face, before me now;
Strangely, like life, I almost see
The dark curls wave upon thy brow!

This face reveals that poet-life,
Still deepening, still rising higher,
A breathing from thy soul of song,
A glow from out thy heart of fire!

And yet, unlike thy portraiture
I would thy *living* face might be,
For ever, as I gaze on *this*,
Thine eyes are turned away from me.

— GRACE GREENWOOD

299

"You smiled, you spoke"

You smiled, you spoke, and I believed,
By every word and smile deceived.
Another man would hope no more;
Nor hope I what I hoped before:
But let not this last wish be vain;
Deceive, deceive me once again!

— WALTER SAVAGE LANDOR

from Art

"What precious thing are you making fast
   In all these silken lines?
And where and to whom will it go at last?
   Such subtle knots and twines!"

"I am tying up all my love in this,
   With all its hopes and fears,
With all its anguish and all its bliss,
   And its hours as heavy as years.

"I am going to send it afar, afar,
   To I know not where above;
To that sphere beyond the highest star
   Where dwells the soul of my Love.

"But in vain, in vain, would I make it fast
   With countless subtle twines;
Forever its fire breaks out at last,
   And shrivels all the lines."

— JAMES THOMSON

"Silent as spring rain"

Silent as spring rain
on a marsh,
my tears
fall to my sleeves
unheard by him.

— Ono No Komachi

Six O'Clock in Princes Street

In twos and threes, they have not far to roam,
  Crowds that thread eastward, gay of eyes;
Those seek no further than their quiet home,
  Wives, walking westward, slow and wise.

Neither should I go fooling over clouds,
  Following gleams unsafe, untrue,
And tiring after beauty through star-crowds,
  Dared I go side by side with you;

Or be you in the gutter where you stand,
  Pale rain-flawed phantom of the place,
With news of all the nations in your hand,
  And all their sorrows in your face.

— WILFRED OWEN

The Definition of Love

My love is of a birth as rare
As 'tis for object strange and high;
It was begotten by Despair
Upon Impossiblility.

Magnanimous Despair alone
Could show me so divine a thing
Where feeble Hope could ne'er have flown,
But vainly flapp'd its tinsel wing.

And yet quickly might arrive
Where my extended soul is fixt,
But Fate does iron wedges drive,
And always crowds itself betwixt.

For Fate with jealous eye does see
Two perfect loves, nor lets them close;
Their union would her ruin be,
And her tyrannic pow'r depose.

And therefore her decrees of steel
Us as the distant poles have plac'd,
(Though love's whole world on us doth wheel)
Not by themselves to be embrac'd;

Unless the giddy heaven fall,
And earth some new convulsion tear;
And, us to join, the world should all
Be cramp'd into a planisphere.

As lines, so loves oblique may well
Themselves in every angle greet;
But ours so truly parallel,
Though infinite, can never meet.

Therefore the love which us doth bind,
But Fate so enviously debars,
Is the conjunction of the mind,
And opposition of the stars.

— ANDREW MARVELL

This Lady's Cruelty

With how sad steps, O moon, thou climb'st the
  skies!
How silently, and with how wan a face!
What! May it be that even in heavenly place
That busy archer his sharp arrows tries?
Sure, if that long-with-love-acquainted eyes
Can judge of love, thou feel'st a lover's case:
I read it in thy looks; thy languished grace
To me, that feel the like, thy state descries.
Then, even of fellowship, O Moon, tell me,
Is constant love deemed there but want of wit?
Are beauties there as proud as here they be?
Do they above love to be loved, and yet
    Those lovers scorn whom that love doth
  possess?
    Do they call "virtue" there—ungratefulness?

— SIR PHILIP SIDNEY

Helene

I walk by day, I wake by night
Thirsting, panting for your beauty—
And ever, ever at my side
There stalks a spectre men call Duty.

I turn aside, I turn about,
And still love beckons, burning bright—
And ever, ever facing me
There hands a sword that men call Right.

I fight the battle in my heart,
And wavering is the victory;
And then I pray to God for strength,
In this, my own Gethsemane.

Oft in my agony of soul
I wonder if God hears my prayers,
And—may He now forgive the thought—
I sometimes wonder if God cares.

— JAMES WELDON JOHNSON

Sometimes with One I Love

Sometimes with one I love I fill myself with rage
   for fear I effuse unreturn'd love,
But now I think there is no unreturn'd love, the
   pay is certain one way or another
(I loved a certain person ardently and my love was
   not return'd,
Yet out of that I have written these songs).

— WALT WHITMAN

My Pretty Rose Tree

A flower was offered to me,
Such a flower as May never bore;
But I said "I've a Pretty Rose-tree,"
And I passed the sweet flower o'er.

Then I went to my Pretty Rose-tree,
To tend her by day and by night;
But my Rose turned away with jealousy,
And her thorns were my only delight.

— WILLIAM BLAKE

Mirage

The hope I dreamed of was a dream,
　Was but a dream; and now I wake,
Exceeding comfortless, and worn, and old,
　For a dream's sake.

I hang my harp upon a tree,
　A weeping willow in a lake;
I hang my silenced harp there, wrung and snapt
　For a dream's sake.

Lie still, lie still, my breaking heart;
　My silent heart, lie still and break:
Life, and the world, and mine own self, are
　changed
　　For a dream's sake.

— Christina Rossetti

*Passionate
Love*

I Love You

I love your lips when they're wet with wine
   And red with a wild desire;
I love your eyes when the lovelight lies
   Lit with a passionate fire.
I love your arms when the warm white flesh
   Touches mine in a fond embrace;
I love your hair when the strands enmesh
   Your kisses against my face.

Not for me the cold, calm kiss
   Of a virgin's bloodless love;
Not for me the saint's white bliss,
   Nor the heart of a spotless dove.
But give me the love that so freely gives
   And laughs at the whole world's blame,
With your body so young and warm in my arms,
   It sets my poor heart aflame.

So kiss me sweet with your warm wet mouth,
   Still fragrant with ruby wine,
And say with a fervor born of the South
   That your body and soul are mine.
Clasp me close in your warm young arms,
   While the pale stars shine above,
And we'll live our whole young lives away
   In the joys of a living love.

— ELLA WHEELER WILCOX

from *The Song of Solomon*

My beloved spake, and said unto me, Rise up, my
love, my fair one, and come away.
For lo, the winter is past, the rain is over and
gone;
The flowers appear on the earth; the time of the
singing of birds is come, and the voice of the
turtle is heard in our land:
The fig tree putteth forth her green figs, and the
vines with the tender grape give a good smell.
Arise, my love, my fair one, and come away.
O my dove, that art in the clefts of the rock, in
the secret places of the stairs, let me see thy
countenance, let me hear thy voice; for sweet
is thy voice, and thy countenance is comely.
Take us the foxes, the little foxes, that spoil the
vines; for our vines have tender grapes.
My beloved is mine, and I am his: he feedeth
among the lilies.
Until the day break, and the shadows flee away,
turn, my beloved, and be thou like a roe or a
young hart upon the mountains of Bether.

— *from* THE AUTHORIZED VERSION

Desire

Where true Love burns Desire is Love's pure flame;
It is the reflex of our earthly frame,
That takes its meaning from the nobler part,
And but translates the language of the heart.

— Samuel Taylor Coleridge

The Wine of Love

The wine of Love is music,
   And the feast of Love is song:
And when Love sits down to the banquet,
   Love sits long:

Sits long and ariseth drunken,
   But not with the feast and the wine;
He reeleth with his own heart,
   That great rich Vine.

— JAMES THOMSON

I Knew a Woman

I knew a woman, lovely in her bones,
When small birds sighed, she would sigh back at
  them;
Ah, when she moved, she moved more ways than
  one:
The shapes a bright container can contain!
Of her choice virtues only gods should speak,
Or English poets who grew up on Greek
(I'd have them sing in chorus, cheek to cheek).

How well her wishes went! She stroked my chin,
She taught me Turn, and Counter-turn, and
  Stand;
She taught me Touch, that undulant white skin;
I nibbled meekly from her proffered hand;
She was the sickle; I, poor I, the rake,
Coming behind her for her pretty sake
(But what prodigious mowing we did make).

Love likes a gander, and adores a goose:
Her full lips pursed, the errant note to seize;
She played it quick, she played it light and loose,
My eyes, they dazzled at her flowing knees;
Her several parts would keep a pure repose,
Or one hip quiver with a mobile nose
(She moved in circles, and those circles moved).

Let seed be grass, and grass turn into hay:
I'm martyr to a motion not my own;
What's freedom for? To know eternity.
I swear she cast a shadow white as stone.
But who would count eternity in days?
These old bones live to learn her wanton ways:
(I measure time by how a body sways).

— THEODORE ROETHKE

Did Not

'Twas a new feeling—something more
Than we had dared to own before,
   Which then we hid not;
We saw it in each other's eye,
And wished, in every half-breathed sigh,
   To speak, but did not.

She felt my lips' impassioned touch—
'Twas the first time I dared so much,
   And yet she chid not;
But whispered o'er by burning brow,
"Oh, do you doubt I love you now?"
   Sweet soul! I did not.

Warmly I felt her bosom thrill,
I pressed it closer, closer still,
   Though gently bid not;
Till—oh! the world hath seldom heard
Of lovers, who so nearly erred,
   And yet, who did not.

— Thomas Moore

"And forgive us our trepasses"

How prone we are to sin; how sweet were made
The pleasures our resistless hearts invade.
Of all my crimes, the breach of all thy laws,
Love, soft bewitching love, has been the cause.
Of all the paths that vanity has trod,
That sure will soonest be forgiven by God.
If things on earth may be to heaven resembled,
It must be love, pure, constant, undissembled.
But if to sin by chance the charmer press,
Forgive, O Lord, forgive our trespasses.

— APHRA BEHN

The Silent Lover

Passions are liken'd best to floods and streams:
The shallow murmur, but the deep are dumb;
So, when affection yields discourse, it seems
    The bottom is but shallow whence they come.
They that are rich in words, in words discover
That they are poor in that which makes a lover.

— SIR WALTER RALEIGH

"Still to be neat, still to be drest"

Still to be neat, still to be drest,
As you were going to a feast;
Still to be powder'd, still perfum'd:
Lady, it is to be presum'd,
Though art's hid causes are not found,
All is not sweet, all is not sound.

Give me a look, give me a face,
That make simplicity a grace;
Robes loosely flowing, hair as free:
Such sweet neglect more taketh me
Than all th'adulteries of art.
They strike mine eyes, but not my heart.

— BEN JONSON

My Love in Her Attire

My love in her attire doth show her wit,
  It doth so well become her:
For every season she hath dressings fit,
  For winter, spring, and summer.
  No beauty she doth miss,
  When all her robes are on:
  But Beauty's self she is,
  When all her robes are gone.

— ANONYMOUS

"*Sweet Cupid,
ripen her desire*"

Sweet Cupid, ripen her desire,
   Thy joyful harvest may begin;
If age approach a little nigher,
   'Twill be too late to get it in.

Cold winter storms lay standing corn,
   Which once too ripe will never rise,
And lovers wish themselves unborn,
   When all their joys lie in their eyes.

Then, sweet, let us embrace and kiss.
   Shall beauty shale upon the ground?
If age bereave us of this bliss,
   Then will no more such sport be found.

— ANONYMOUS

Song to Amarantha, That She Would Dishevel Her Hair

Amarantha sweet and fair
Ah braid no more that shining hair!
As my curious hand or eye
Hovering round thee let it fly.

Let it fly as unconfin'd
As its calm ravisher, the wind,
Who hath left his darling th'East,
To wanton o'er that spicy nest.

Ev'ry tress must be confest
But neatly tangled at the best;
Like a clue of golden thread,
Most excellently ravelled.

Do not then wind up that light
In ribands, and o'er-cloud in night;
Like the sun in's early ray,
But shake your head and scatter day.

See 'tis broke! Within this grove
The bower, and the walks of love,
   Weary lie we down and rest,
And fan each other's panting breast.

   Here we'll strip and cool our fire
In cream below, in milk-baths higher:
   And when all wells are drawn dry,
I'll drink a tear out of thine eye,

   Which our very joys shall leave
That sorrows thus we can deceive;
   Or our very sorrows weep,
That joys so ripe, so little keep.

— RICHARD LOVELACE

In the Orchard

Leave go my hands, let me catch breath and see;
Let the dew-fall drench either side of me;
    Clear apple-leaves are soft upon that moon;
Seen sidelong like a blossom in the tree;
    And God, ah God, that day should be so soon.

The grass is thick and cool, it lets us lie.
Kissed upon either cheek and either eye,
    I turn to thee as some green afternoon
Turns toward sunset, and is loth to die;
    Ah God, ah God, that day should be so soon.

Lie closer, lean your face upon my side,
Feel where the dew fell that has hardly dried,
    Hear how the blood beats that went nigh to
    swoon;
The pleasure lives there when the sense has died,
    Ah God, ah God, that day should be so soon.

O my fair lord, I charge you leave me this:
It is not sweeter than a foolish kiss?
    Nay take it then, my flower, my first in June,
My rose, so like a tender mouth it is:
    Ah God, ah God, that day should be so soon.

Love, till dawn sunder night from day with fire
Dividing my delight and my desire,
  The crescent life and love the plenilune,
Love me though dusk begin and dark retire;
  Ah God, ah God, that day should be so soon.

Ah, my heart fails, my blood draws back; I know,
When life runs over, life is near to go;
  And with the slain of love love's ways are
  strewn,
And with their blood, if love will have it so;
  Ah God, ah God, that day should be so soon.

Ah, do thy will now; slay me if thou wilt;
There is no building now the walls are built,
  No quarrying now the corner-stone is hewn,
No drinking now the vine's whole blood is spilt;
  Ah God, ah God, that day should be so soon.

Nay, slay me now; nay, for I will be slain;
Pluck thy red pleasure from the teeth of pain,
   Break down thy vine ere yet grape-gatherers
  prune,
Slay me ere day can slay desire again;
   Ah God, ah God, that day should be so soon.

Yea, with thy sweet lips, with thy sweet sword;
  yea
Take life and all, for I will die, I say;
   Love, I gave love, is life a better boon?
For sweet night's sake I will not live till day;
   Ah God, ah God, that day should be so soon.

Nay, I will sleep then only; nay, but go.
Ah sweet, too sweet to me, my sweet, I know
   Love, sleep, and death go to the sweet tune;
Hold my hair fast, and kiss me through it soon.
   Ah God, ah God, that day should be so soon.

—A. C. SWINBURNE

Renouncement

I must not think of thee; and, tired yet strong,
I shun the thought that lurks in all delight—
  The thought of thee—and in the blue
  heavens's height,
And in the sweetest passage of a song.
Oh, just beyond the fairest thoughts that throng
  This breast, the thought of thee waits hidden
  yet bright;
But it must never, never come in sight;
I must stop short of thee the whole day long.

But when sleep comes to close each difficult day,
  When night gives pause to the long watch I
  keep,
And all my bonds I needs must loose apart,
Must doff my will as raiment laid away,—
  With the first dream that comes with the first
  sleep
I run, I run, I am gathered to thy heart.

— ALICE MEYNELL

The Dream

All trembling in my arms Aminta lay,
Defending of the bliss I strove to take;
Raising my rapture by her kind delay,
Her force so charming was and weak.
The soft resistance did betray the grant,
While I pressed on the heaven of my desires;
Her rising breasts with nimbler motions pant;
Her dying eyes assume new fires.
Now to the height of languishment she grows,
And still her looks new charms put on;
Now the last mystery of Love she knows,
We sigh, and kiss: I waked, and all was done.

'Twas but a dream, yet by my heart I knew,
Which still was panting, part of it was true:
Oh how I strove the rest to have believed;
Ashamed and angry to be undeceived!

— APHRA BEHN

331

Mediocrity
in Love Rejected

Give me more love, or more disdain;
 The torrid or the frozen zone
Bring equal ease unto my pain;
 The temperate affords me none:
Either extreme, of love or hate,
Is sweeter than a calm estate.

Give me a storm; if it be love,
 Like Danaë in that golden shower,
I swim in pleasure; if it prove
 Disdain, that torrent will devour
My vulture hopes; and he's possessed
Of heaven that's but from hell released.
 Then crown my joys, or cure my pain;
 Give me more love or more disdain.

— Thomas Carew

"Wild Nights—
Wild Nights!"

Wild Nights—Wild Nights!
Were I with thee
Wild Nights should be
Our luxury!

Futile—the Winds—
To a Heart in port—
Done with the Compass—
Done with the Chart!

Rowing in Eden—
Ah, the Sea!
Might I but moor—Tonight—
In Thee!

— EMILY DICKINSON

"I cry your mercy"

I cry your mercy—pity—love!—aye, love!
   Merciful love that tantalizes not,
One-thoughted, never-wandering, guileless love,
   Unmasked, and being seen—without a blot!
O! let me have thee whole,—all—all—be mine!
   That shape, that fairness, that sweet minor zest
Of love, your kiss,—those hands, those eyes divine,
   That warm, white, lucent, million-pleasured breast,
Yourself—your soul—in pity give me all,
   Withhold no atom's atom or I die
Or living on perhaps, your wretched thrall,
   Forget, in the mist of idle misery,
Life's purposes,—the palate of my mind
   Losing its gust, and my ambition blind!

— JOHN KEATS

334

Now!

Out of your whole life give but a moment!
   All of your life that has gone before,
   All to come after it,—so you ignore,
So you make perfect the present; condense,
In a rapture of rage, for perfection's endowment,
Thought and feeling and soul and sense,
Merged in a moment which gives me at last
You around me for once, you beneath me, above
  me—
Me, sure that, despite of time future, time past,
This tick of life-time's one moment you love me!
How long such suspension may linger? Ah, Sweet,
   The moment eternal—just that and no
     more—
   When ecstasy's utmost we clutch at the core,
While cheeks burn, arms open, eyes shut, and
  lips meet!

— ROBERT BROWNING

335

New Year's Eve

There are only two things now,
The great black night scooped out
And this fireglow.

This fireglow, the core,
And we the two ripe pips
That are held in store.

Listen, the darkness rings
As it circulates round our fire.
Take off your things.

Your shoulders, your bruised throat!
Your breasts, your nakedness!
This fiery coat!

As the darkness flickers and dips,
As the firelight falls and leaps
From your feet to your lips!

— D. H. LAWRENCE

Elegy 5

In summer's heat and mid-time of the day
To rest my limbs upon a bed I lay,
One window shut, the other open stood,
Which gave such light, as twinkles in a wood,
Like twilight glimpse at setting of the sun,
Or night being past, and yet not day begun.
Such light to shamefast maidens must be shown,
Where they must sport, and seem to be
  unknown.
Then came Corinna in a long loose gown,
Her white neck hid the tresses hanging down:
Resembling fair Semiramis going to bed
Or Layis of a thousand wooers sped.
I snatched her gown, being thin, the harm was
  small,

Yet strived she to be covered there withal.
And striving thus as one that would be cast,
Betrayed herself, and yielded at the last.
Stark naked as she stood before mine eye,
Not one wen in her body could I spy.
What arms and shoulders did I touch and see,
How apt her breasts were to be pressed by me.
How smooth a belly under her waist saw I?
How large a leg, and what a lusty thigh?
To leave the rest, all liked me passing well,
I clinged her naked body, down she fell,
Judge you the rest, being tired she bade me kiss,
Jove send me more such afternoons as this.

— OVID
translated by CHRISTOPHER MARLOWE

To His Mistress Going to Bed

Come, Madam, come, all rest my powers defy,
Until I labour, I in labour lie.
The foe oft-times, having the foe in sight,
Is tired with standing, though they never fight.
Off with that girdle, like heaven's zone glistering
But a far fairer world encompassing.
Unpin that spangled breast-plate, which you wear
That th'eyes of busy fools may be stopped there:
Unlace yourself, for that harmonious chime
Tells me from you that now 'tis your bed time.
Off with that happy busk, whom I envy
That still can be, and still can stand so nigh.
Your gown's going off such beauteous state reveals
As when from flowery meads th'hills shadow steals.
Off with your wiry coronet and show
The hairy diadem which on you doth grow.
Off with those shoes: and then safely tread
In this love's hallowed temple, this soft bed.
In such white robes heaven's angels used to be
Received by men; thou Angel bring'st with thee
A heaven like Mahomet's Paradise; and though
Ill spirits walk in white, we easily know
By this these Angels from an evil sprite:
They set out hairs, but these the flesh upright.

Licence my roving hands, and let them go
Behind, before, above, between, below.
Oh my America, my new found land,
My kingdom, safeliest when with one man
   manned,
My mine of precious stones, my Empery,
How blessed am I in this discovering thee.
To enter in these bonds is to be free,
Then where my hand is set my seal shall be.
   Full nakedness, all joys are due to thee.
As souls unbodied, bodies unclothed must be
To taste whole joys. Gems which you women use
Are as Atlanta's balls, cast in men's views,
That when a fool's eye lighteth on a gem
His earthly soul may covet theirs not them.
Like pictures, or like books' gay coverings made
For laymen, are all women thus arrayed;
Themselves are mystic books, which only we
Whom their imputed grace will dignify
Must see revealed. Then since I may know,
As liberally as to a midwife show
Thyself; cast all, yea this white linen hence.
Here is no penance, must less innocence.
   To teach thee, I am naked first: Why then
What need'st thou have more covering than a man.

— JOHN DONNE

Knee Song

Being kissed on the back
of the knee is a moth
at the windowscreen and
yes my darling a dot
on the fathometer is
tinkerbelle with her cough
and twice I will give up my
honor and stars will stick
like tacks in the night
yes oh yes yes yes two
little snails at the back
of the knee building bon-
fires something like eye-
lashes something two zippos
striking yes yes yes small
and me maker.

— ANNE SEXTON

i like my body
when it is with your body

i like my body when it is with your
body. It is so quite new a thing.
Muscles better and nerves more.
i like your body.   i like what it does,
i like its hows.   i like to feel the spine
of your body and its bones,and the trembling
-firm-smooth ness and which i will
again and again and again
kiss, i like kissing this and that of you,
i like,slowly stroking the,shocking fuzz
of your electric fur,and what-is-it comes
over parting flesh....And eyes big love-crumbs,

and possibly i like the thrill

of under me you so quite new

— e. e. cummings

How Gentle

how gentle are we rising
easy as eyes in sockets turning

intimate the hardness: jaw
upon jaw, forehead warm

upon forehead
kisses quick as breaths, without volition

Love: I am luminous
careless as love's breathing

fluorescent glowing the fine
warm veins and bones

your weight,
the sky lowered suddenly

I am loved: a message
clanging of a bell in silence

you are quickened with surprise
our horizons surrender to walls

Are we wearing out
our skins' defenses?—

turning to silk, texture of flashy
airy surfaces scant as breaths?

I am loved: the noon slides gently
suddenly upon us
to wake us

— JOYCE CAROL OATES

"In this world"

In this world,
love has no color—
yet how deeply
my body
is stained by yours.

— IZUMI SHIKIBU

Tender
Love

Where Does This Tenderness Come From?

Where does this tenderness come from?
These are not the—first curls I
have stroked slowly—and lips I
have known are—darker than yours

as stars rise often and go out again
(where does this tenderness come from?)
so many eyes have risen and died out
   in front of these eyes of mine.

and yet no such song have
I heard in the darkness of night before,
(where does this tenderness come from?):
   here, on the ribs of the singer.

Where does this tenderness come from?
And what shall I do with it, young
sly singer, just passing by?
Your lashes are—longer than anyone's.

— MARINA TSVETAEVA
translated by ELAINE FEINSTEIN

A Poem
of Friendship

We are not lovers
because of the love
we make
but the love
we have

We are not friends
because of the laughs
we spend
but the tears
we save

I don't want to be near you
for the thoughts we share
but the words we never have
to speak

I will never miss you
because of what we do
but what we are
together

— NIKKI GIOVANNI

Aubade

Stay, O sweet, and do not rise,
The light that shines comes from thine eyes;
The day breaks not, it is my heart,
Because that you and I must part.
  Stay, or else my joys will die,
  And perish in their infancy.

— ANONYMOUS

Sudden Light

I have been here before,
　　But when or how I cannot tell:
I know the grass beyond the door,
　　The sweet keen smell,
The sighing sound, the lights around the shore.

You have been mine before,—
　　How long ago I may not know:
But just when at the swallow's soar
　　Your neck turn'd so,
Some veil did fall,—I knew it all of yore.

Has this been thus before?
　　And shall not thus time's eddying flight
Still with our lives our love restore
　　In death's despite,
And day and night yield one delight once more?

— DANTE GABRIEL ROSSETTI

She

I think the dead are tender. Shall we kiss?—
My lady laughs, delighting in what is.
If she but sighs, a bird puts out its tongue.
She makes space lonely with a lovely song.
She lilts a low soft language, and I hear
Down long sea-chambers of the inner ear.

We sing together; we sing mouth to mouth.
The garden is a river flowing south.
She cries out loud the soul's own secret joy;
She dances, and the ground bears her away.
She knows the speech of light, and makes it plain
A lively thing can come to life again.

I feel her presence in the common day,
In that slow dark that widens every eye.
She moves as water moves, and comes to me,
Stayed by what was, and pulled by what would be.

— THEODORE ROETHKE

Love's Emblems

There was a rose, that blushing grew
Within my life's young bower;
The angels sprinkled holy dew
Upon the blessed flower.
I glory to resign it, love,
Though it was dear to me;
Amid thy laurels twine it, love,
It only blooms for thee.

There was a rich and radiant gem
I long kept hid from sight;
Lost from some seraph's diadem,
It shone with heaven's own light!
The world could never tear it, love,
That gem of gems, from me;
Yet on thy fond breast wear it, love,
It only shines for thee.

There was a bird came to my breast,
When I was very young;
I only knew that sweet bird's nest,
To me she only sung.
But, ah! one summer day, love,
I saw that bird depart!
The truant flew thy way, love,
And nestled in thy heart!

— GRACE GREENWOOD

"When in disgrace with Fortune and men's eyes"

When in disgrace with Fortune and men's eyes,
I all alone beweep my outcast state,
And trouble deaf heaven with my bootless cries,
And look upon myself and curse my fate,
Wishing me like to one more rich in hope,
Featured like him, like him with friends
  possessed,
Desiring this man's art, and that man's scope,
With what I most enjoy contented least;
Yet in these thoughts myself almost despising,
Haply I think on thee, and then my state,
Like to the lark at break of day arising
From sullen earth, sings hymns at heaven's gate;
  For thy sweet love rememb'red such wealth
  brings,
  That then I scorn to change my state with
  kings.

— WILLIAM SHAKESPEARE

My Star

All that I know
Of a certain star,
Is, it can throw
(Like the angled spar)
Now a dart of red,
Now a dart of blue,
Till my friends have said
They would fain see, too,
My star that dartles the red and the blue!

Then it stops like a bird; like a flower, hangs
  furled:
    They must solace themselves with the Saturn
  above it.
What matter to me if their star is a world?
    Mine has opened its soul to me; therefore I
  love it.

— ROBERT BROWNING

356

The Presence of Love

And in Life's noisiest hour,
There whipsers still the ceaseless Love of Thee,
The heart's *Self-solace* and soliloquy.

You mould my Hopes, you fashion me within;
And to the leading Love-throb in the Heart
Thro' all my Being, thro' my pulses beat;
You lie in all my many Thoughts, like Light,
Like the fair light of Dawn, or summer Eve
On rippling Stream, or cloud-reflecting Lake.
And looking to the Heaven, that bends above you,
How oft! I bless the Lot, that made me love you.

— SAMUEL TAYLOR COLERIDGE

If Ever I Have Thought or Said

If ever I have thought or said
In all the seasons of the past
One word at which thy heart has bled
Believe me, it will be the last.

The tides of life are deep and wide,
The currents swift to bear apart
E'en kindred ships; but from thy side
I pray my sail may never start.

If, in the turning day and night
Of this our earth, our little year,
Thou shalt have lost me from thy sight
Across the checkered spaces drear,

Thy words are uttered; and the mind
Accustomed, cannot all forget;
While written in my heart I find
An impulse that is deeper yet.

We love but never know the things,
To value them, that nearest stand.
The heart that travels seaward brings
The dearest treasure home to land.

— PHILIP HENRY SAVAGE

Watching You

for Joy

I watch you
from the gentle slope
where it is warm
by your shoulder.
My eyes are closed.
I can feel the tap
of your blood
against my cheek.
Inside my mind,
I see the gentle move
ment of your valleys,
the undulations
of slow turnings.

Opening my eyes,
there is a soft dark
and beautiful butte
moving up and then down
as you breathe.
There are fine
and very tiny ferns
growing, and I can
make them move
by breathing.
I watch you with my skin
moving upon yours,
and I have known you well.

— SIMON J. ORTIZ

Winter Love

Let us have winter loving that the heart
May be in peace and ready to partake
Of the slow pleasure spring would wish to hurry
Or that in summer harshly would awake,
And let us fall apart, O gladly weary,
The white skin shaken like a white snowflake.

— ELIZABETH JENNINGS

from *The Princess*

Now sleeps the crimson petal, now the white;
Nor waves the cypress in the palace walk;
Nor winks the gold fin in the porphyry font:
The fire-fly wakens: waken thou with me.

Now droops the milkwhite peacock like a ghost,
And like a ghost she glimmers on to me.

Now lies the Earth all Danaë to the stars,
And all thy heart lies open unto me.

Now slides the silent meteor on, and leaves
A shining furrow, as thy thoughts in me.

Now folds the lily all her sweetness up,
And slips into the bosom of the lake:
So fold thyself, my dearest, thou, and slip
Into my bosom and be lost in me.

— ALFRED LORD TENNYSON

To Jane

The keen stars were twinkling,
And the fair moon was rising among them,
    Dear Jane.
The guitar was tinkling,
    But the notes were not sweet till you sung them
    Again.

    As the moon's soft splendour
O'er the faint cold starlight of Heaven
        Is thrown,
    So your voice most tender
To the strings without soul had then given
    Its own.

The stars will awaken,
Though the moon sleep a full hour later
   To-night;
   No leaf will be shaken
Whilst the dews of your melody scatter
   Delight.

Though the sound overpowers,
Sing again, with your dear voice revealing
   A tone

Of some world far from ours,
Where music and moonlight and feeling
   Are one.

— PERCY BYSSHE SHELLEY

When I Heard
at the Close of Day

When I heard at the close of day how my name
  had been receiv'd with plaudits in the capitol,
  still it was not a happy night for me that
  follow'd,
And else when I carous'd, or when my plans were
  accomplish'd, still I was not happy,
But the day when I rose at dawn from the bed of
  perfect health, refresh'd, singing, inhaling the
  ripe breath of autumn,
When I saw the full moon in the west grow pale
  and disappear in the morning light,
When I wander'd alone over the beach, and
  undressing bathed, laughing with the cool
  waters, and saw the sun rise,
And when I thought how my dear friend my lover
  was on his way coming, O then I was happy,
O then each breath tasted sweeter, and all that
  day my food nourish'd me more, and the
  beautiful day pass'd well,
And the next came with equal joy, and with the
  next at evening came my friend,

And that night while all was still I heard the
    waters roll slowly continually up the shores,
I heard the hissing rustle of the liquid and sands
    as directed to me whispering to congratulate
    me,
For the one I love most lay sleeping by me under
    the same cover in the cool night,
In the stillness in the autumn moonbeams his
    face was inclined toward me,
And his arm lay lightly around my breast—and
    that night I was happy.

— WALT WHITMAN

Lullaby

Lay your sleeping head, my love,
Human on my faithless arm;
Time and fevers burn away
Individual beauty from
Thoughtful children, and the grave
Proves the child ephemeral:
But in my arms till break of day
Let the living creature lie,
Mortal, guilty, but to me
The entirely beautiful.

Soul and body have no bounds:
To lovers as they lie upon
Her tolerant enchanted slope
In their ordinary swoon,
Grave the vision Venus sends
Of supernatural sympathy,
Universal love and hope;
While an abstract insight wakes
Among the glaciers and the rocks
The hermit's carnal ecstasy.

Certainty, fidelity
On the stroke of midnight pass
Like vibrations of a bell
And fashionable madmen raise
Their pedantic boring cry:
Every farthing of the cost,
All the dreaded cards foretell,
Shall be paid, but not from this night
Not a whisper, not a thought,
Not a kiss nor look be lost.

Beauty, midnight, vision dies:
Let the winds of dawn that blow
Softly round your dreaming head
Such a day of welcome show
Eye and knocking heart may bless,
Find our mortal world enough;
Noons of dryness find you fed
By the involuntary powers,
Nights of insult let you pass
Watched by every human love.

W. H. AUDEN

Serenade

So sweet the hour, so calm the time,
I feel it more than half a crime,
When Nature sleeps and stars are mute,
To mar the silence ev'n with lute.
At rest on ocean's brilliant dyes
An image of Elysium lies:
Seven Pleaiades entranced in Heaven,
Form in the deep another seven:
Endymion nodding from above
Sees in the sea a second love.
Within the valleys dim and brown,
And on the spectral mountain's crown,
The wearied light is dying down,
And earth, and stars, and sea, and sky
Are redolent of sleep, as I
Am redolent of thee and thine
Enthralling love, my Adeline.

— EDGAR ALLAN POE

A Woman's
Last Word

Let's contend no more, Love,
    Strive nor weep:
All be as before, Love,
    —Only sleep!

What so wild as words are?
    I and thou
In debate, as birds are,
    Hawk on bough!

See the creature stalking
    While we speak!
Hush and hide the talking,
    Cheek on cheek!

What so false as truth is,
    False to thee?
Where the serpent's tooth is,
    Shun the tree—

Where the apple reddens
    Never pry—
Lest we lose our Edens
    Eve and I.

Be a god and hold me
  With a charm!
Be a man and fold me
  With thine arm!

Teach me, only teach, Love!
    As I ought.
I will speak thy speech, Love,
    Think thy thought—

Meet, if thou require it,
    Both demands,
Laying flesh and spirit
    In thy hands.

That shall be tomorrow,
    Not tonight;
I must bury sorrow
    Out of sight:

—Must a little weep, Love,
    (Foolish me!)
And so fall asleep, Love,
    Loved by thee.

— ROBERT BROWNING

Index of Authors

Index of Titles

Index of First Lines

387